Lektürehilfen

Jeannette Walls

Half Broke Horses

von Sarah Nowotny

Klett Lerntraining

Sarah Nowotny kommt aus London und hat langjährige Erfahrung als Lehrerin. Sie ist als freie Autorin und Übersetzerin tätig.

Die Textzitate folgen der Ausgabe:
Jeannette Walls. Half Broke Horses. A true-life novel. Ernst Klett Sprachen. Stuttgart 2013. ISBN 978-3-12-579888-5

9 783129 230824

Auflage 4. 3. 2. 1. | 2016 2015 2014 2013
Die letzten Zahlen bezeichnen jeweils die Auflage und das Jahr des Druckes.

Redaktion: Günter Maier
Umschlagfoto: Corbis (Lynn Goldsmith), Düsseldorf
Illustration und Grafik: Martin Lay
Satz: DOPPELPUNKT, Stuttgart
Druck: Beltz Bad Langensalza GmbH
Printed in Germany
ISBN: 978-3-12-923082-4

Contents

The Story 5

I Salt Draw 5
II The Miraculous Staircase 8
III Promises 13
IV The Red Silk Shirt 23
V Lambs 30
VI Teacher Lady 42
VII The Garden of Eden 49
VIII Gumshoes 58
IX The Flyboy 63
EPILOGUE The Little Critter 67

The Characters 69

Lily Casey Smith 69
Mom 78
Dad 81
Buster 85
Helen 86
Ted Conover 87
Jim Smith 89
Rosemary 92
Little Jim 99
Rex Walls 100
Mother Albertina 104
Minnie 105
Rooster 107

Themes and Motifs 109

Ranch life versus city life 109
Education and teaching. 116
Religion. 120
Horses. 124
Cars and planes 126
Playing the cards you've been dealt 129

About the author 131

Bibliography 133

Model Questions and Answers. 134

1 "Let that be a lesson to you" 134
2. "Most important thing in life is learning how to fall" 136
3. Lily's relationships with women 139
4. What are "half-broke horses"? 143
5. Role of teaching 146
6. Lily's two husbands. 149
7. "Lily's distinctive voice" 152

Index 154

The Story

I Salt Draw

➟ Lily saves her brother and sister from the flash flood. ➟ First impressions of her parents. ➟ Life in the dugout on Salt Draw. ➟ The family lose their home and move to New Mexico.	Salt Draw

"Half Broke Horses" opens with a dramatic event: a flash flood. Lily Casey, the protagonist, then aged 10, saves herself, her brother Buster and her sister Helen from drowning. Realizing that the flood is approaching too quickly for them to get home safely, she makes them climb into a tree, and keeps them awake all night by having them recite lists of things they have learnt, such as the names of presidents. Thanks to Lily's resourcefulness, the siblings survive the night and are able to make their way back home the next morning. Their parents' reactions to their safe return are quite different: their father is delighted to see them and immediately comes out to greet them. Their mother, on the other hand, gets down on her knees to give thanks to God for saving her children. She also takes credit for saving them, as she has been up all night praying for them. Although Buster and Helen join their mother in prayer, Lily remains skeptical, firmly believing that she was the one who saved them, not her mother's prayer or a "guardian angel". Her father's perspective, however, is quite simply: "maybe that angel was you" (pg. 16).

First indication of Lily's determination and survival instinct

Different reactions of their parents

Lily and her family live a hard life on their homestead on Salt Draw, although things are easier for them than for some of the other settlers as their land has direct access to water. They keep different kinds of animals, such as cows and hens, but their father's main job is breeding and training carriage horses. He loves horses, even though his disabilities (a severe speech impediment and limited use of the right side of his body) mean

Salt Draw is a river in Texas

Dad's disabilities were caused by a horse kicking him in the head when he was three

he cannot actually ride them himself. However, he is still able to train them, and is at his happiest when working with horses. He finds dealing with people far more difficult, partly because of his "terrible temper" (pg. 25), and partly due to frustration because they cannot understand what he is saying. He also spends a lot of time fighting lawsuits with his relatives as he believes he has been cheated out of his inheritance.

Lily's first home

Lily was born in 1901 in a dugout, a typical type of home for the region that was literally dug out of the mud by the riverbank. Due to the lack of wood available for building, it was a good solution, although dugouts came with several disadvantages, such as insects and other animals breaking through the walls and roof or, in summer, huge numbers of mosquitoes. Worst of all, a dugout could not survive extremely bad weather conditions, as the family discovered during another flood. Despite the efforts of Lily and the two family servants, Apache and Lupe, their home collapses.

However, after the flood, the family discovers that one of their neighbors has moved back to Cleveland, unable to put up with the hardships of living on Salt Draw any more. This neighbor abandons his wooden house, the remains of which Lily's family takes and uses to build their own house of wood. They now have a proper home for the first time.

Mom – a lady

Lily's parents are very different from each other. Her mother is a delicate, well-bred woman, "a lady" (pg. 23) as her father puts it. She does not really like living on Salt Draw, but does her best to add a civilized touch to their dugout with furniture and ornaments. She also tries to make sure her children remain genteel, and one of her greatest concerns is finding husbands for her daughters. When it comes to doing the hard work necessary to run their ranch, she is not of much practical use, tending to turn to prayer in times of crisis rather than helping out. This, in addition to the fact that her father is physically disabled and is often away from home anyway, means it is often left up to Lily to make sure things get done. Her mother has mixed feelings about this: on the one hand, she relies on her daughter, but worries that her unladylike behavior will make it more difficult for her to attract a man.

Whereas Mom concentrates on ensuring that her children are brought up well, it is their father who gives them an education. As he does not think much of the teaching standards at the local school, he teaches Lily himself, who then passes on what she has learnt to her brother and sister. In addition to this, Dad teaches Lily how to train horses. Her main job is breaking the horses, in other words, teaching them to accept being handled and then ridden by a human. She is quite fearless, and often gets thrown, once breaking her arm very badly. Her mother is horrified, and does not think a young girl should be breaking horses. Her father, however, knows that she will carry on, and that she has learnt something from her experience: "Most important thing in life [...] is learning how to fall" (pg. 38).

Learning to break horses

When Lily is eleven, the family's home is struck by a tornado. Although these were, common in the region, most of them were fairly harmless. In this particular case, however, Lily and her father can sense from the horses' behavior that something bad is about to happen. They set the horses free, then join the rest of the family, who are taking cover under the house. Lily is so frightened that even she joins in her mother's prayers in the hope that they will survive. They do, but their house is destroyed by a nearby windmill, which has fallen onto the roof. Dad decides that it is time to pack up the belongings they have managed to save and move back to his family's ranch in New Mexico. Lily has mixed feelings about leaving. On the one hand, it feels as if they are giving up like so many of the easterners who come to settle in this part of Texas and find life too tough. She loves the land, as it is the only place she has known up to now. On the other hand, she accepts that they cannot go on living there, as they have lost their home. This time, she even agrees with her mother that everything is God's will. It seems to her that God is telling them it is time to move on.

Moving to New Mexico

II The Miraculous Staircase

The Miraculous Staircase	
	→ The KC Ranch is very different to the dugout on Salt Draw: it is built on fertile land, which means the family has more farming to do. → Lily goes away to school, but soon has to leave again, despite her academic success, because her father cannot pay the fees. → The principal of the school, Mother Albertina, has a strong influence on her. → Lily takes a teaching test that qualifies her to teach in small remote schools. → At fifteen, she leaves home to work as a teacher.

Contrast of KC Ranch to the dugout

The Casey family's new home, which, because of his theory that words should be spelt phonetically, Dad decides must be known as the "KC Ranch" rather than the "Casey Ranch" (pg. 49), is very different from their old one on Salt Draw. They are now living in a strong house with thick walls, made of adobe and stone. The children are able to sleep in a different room from the adults, as there are two bedrooms. The greatest contrast, however, is the land belonging to the ranch. Instead of the dry, barren landscape of their last home, the land is green and there are crops growing. However, the ranch is also a lot more work than their last home. The fields have to be taken care of, the produce picked and sold at the market, and they need to employ migrant workers to help them.

Dad concentrates on other projects rather than the practicalities of the ranch

Although in theory Dad likes the idea of being a landowner, in practice he often gets distracted by other projects, such as writing a biography of Billy the Kid, who once stopped at the Casey ranch when he was young. Therefore, the running of the ranch is mostly left to Lily.

That year, Lily's brother Buster is sent away to school. Although he is two years younger than her, their parents believe it is more important for him, as a boy, to get some formal education that will allow him to get a job when he is older. Lily, who loves learning, is the one who really wants to go to school, and her parents promise that when she's thirteen she can go to a convent school: the Sisters of Loretto Academy of Our Lady of the

Light in Santa Fe. When the time comes, she and her father travel the two hundred miles from the ranch to Santa Fe together. Having lived in isolated places up until this point, Lily hasn't had much contact with girls of her own age, and is used to telling other people (her siblings, their servants and workers) what to do. Her father gives her lots of advice on how to get along with her peers instead of fighting them, even though he has to admit that he himself is not good at following his own advice.

Dad advises Lily on school life

At the school in Santa Fe, Lily and her father meet Mother Albertina, the Mother Superior of the convent, who will have a strong influence on Lily's life. She shows them around the school, including the chapel which contains the "Miraculous Staircase" (pg. 54). The chapel was originally built without a staircase leading up to the choir loft, so the nuns prayed for help. One day, a man turned up and offered to build a staircase. Nobody knew who he was or what type of wood he used, but he left the nuns with a spiral staircase that was able to stand without support. They believed that the staircase and the circumstances under which it was constructed to be a miracle.

The Miraculous Staircase

Right from the start, Lily likes Mother Albertina. She is always calm yet busy, and treats all of the girls the same, no matter what their background is or how intelligent they are. She also enjoys being at school, and not just because of the opportunities to learn. As she puts it: "I had never had it so easy in my life" (pg. 54-55). Although the pupils have to get up early and have various jobs to do around the school in addition to their lessons, it is much easier than the life of hard physical work on the ranch. Lily does well at school, reads lots of books and helps the weaker students. Many of her fellow pupils are rich, and far more genteel than she is, but she still manages to make some friends. Mother Albertina notices her potential, and talks to her about her future. She tells Lily that she does not have to get married, like most of the girls at the school will do, but even if she does, she should have a career. At that time, women had limited career options: the only real possibilities for them to

Influence of Mother Albertina

work were as a nurse, a secretary or a teacher. Mother Albertina is convinced that Lily, with her strong personality, would make an excellent teacher. This gives Lily something to think about, and she begins to believe that teaching is her Purpose in life.

Lily has to leave school

However, a short time after this conversation, Lily experiences a setback. Mother Albertina gives her the bad news that her father is unable to pay the fees for the second half of the school year, and that she will therefore have to go home. The nun has tried to find a way to allow Lily to stay, but the only option would be for her to agree to become a nun. Lily knows in her heart that religious life is not for her. She is deeply disappointed, and miserable at the thought of having to return to the KC Ranch and spend the rest of her life working there. Mother Albertina, however, is encouraging, and tries to reassure Lily that she has the strength to deal with this disappointment and make her way in life: "When God closes a window, he opens a door. But it's up to you to find it" (pg. 60).

Encouragement from Mother Albertina

When Lily arrives back home, she finds out what has happened to the money for her tuition: her father has spent it on four Great Danes. He is planning to make lots of money by breeding from them. She is, of course, upset that her father has spent the money on dogs, especially as he has not taken Buster out of school. However, her father's attitude is that it was a waste of money to send her to school, as he can teach her everything she needs to know. He then admits the real reason he has made her come home: "we need you on the ranch" (pg. 62). She thinks he may have bought the dogs as an excuse to stop paying for her education, and wonders how she will find the "door" Mother Albertina told her about.

Dad has bought dogs with Lily's tuition fees

The ranch has not been cared for very well while Lily was away, and she spots several jobs that need doing. However, her father does now have extra help in the form of a tenant farmer, Zachary Clemens, who lives with his wife and daughter in an outbuilding. They are extremely poor, but Lily comes to like them, especially Dorothy, the daughter, who is very skilled in practical

The Clemens family

matters and works hard. One day, Dorothy comes to tell them that, while out working on the farm, she has found all four dogs shot dead on the border of their property and their neighbor's. In a rage, Dad gallops off in one of his carriages to confront the neighbor, Old Man Pucket. When he returns, he is even more furious. Old Man Pucket told him that he did kill the dogs because they were on his ranch chasing his cattle. Dad is determined to get his revenge, and runs into the house to get his shotgun. Luckily, Dorothy and Lily intervene. Dorothy is strong enough to take the gun away from Dad: "You can't go killing someone over dogs [...]. That's how feuds get started" (pg. 64). She explains that this is why her family is so poor: her brother killed another man over an argument about a game of horseshoes, and in return that man's cousin killed her brother. The cousin then came to attack her father to stop him from taking revenge, forcing the family to abandon their property and escape to New Mexico. Lily also reminds Dad how his own father was shot dead due to an argument about eight dollars. After a while, Dad calms down, but decides to take Old Man Pucket to court over the matter.

Their neighbor shot the dogs

Dad wants revenge

Dad does a lot of preparation for the trial. Lily is to represent him and Dorothy will be the main witness. He researches his case well and makes sure Lily knows exactly what to say. However, when the case comes to court, the judge is not interested in rhetoric: he simply wants to know what happened. After Lily has told him the facts, he asks Old Man Pucket if he shot the dogs. Old Man Pucket admits that he did, because they were threatening his cattle and looked like wolves from a distance. The judge deals with the case quickly and simply: Dad is reprimanded for keeping such large dogs, but Old Man Pucket is forced to pay compensation, in the form of horses or cows if he does not have enough money. Therefore, a few days later, Old Man Pucket turns up at the KC Ranch with eight horses. As Dad refuses to speak to him, Lily goes out to accept the animals, believing that it is wrong to hold a grudge against a neighbor, as you never know when you might need his help. The horses Old Man Pucket has given them, however, are not worth nearly as much as the dogs. They are all "half-broke horses"

The trial

Their neighbor gives them "half-broke horses"

(pg. 69), probably wild horses that have been used by cowboys for a day or two and then released again, without ever having been properly trained to take a rider. Such horses become afraid of humans because they have been treated so roughly. On the other hand, they are intelligent, brave creatures with potential: "if you broke them right, they made good horses" (pg. 69). There is one that stands out from the rest, a brown, black and white mare, whose obvious intelligence catches Lily's eye. Dad gives her the horse, who she names "Patches" (pg. 70).

Lily's horse Patches

It does not take long for Lily to break Patches properly, and she soon is able to work on the ranch. As well as this, Lily and Patches take part in horse races, some of which they win. The summer after these events, Buster completes the eighth grade at school and comes home. He is not interested in any more education, as he feels he has learnt enough to be able to run the ranch. It soon becomes clear that he is in love with Dorothy. Although their mother does not approve, Lily feels they will make a good couple, especially as Dorothy has the motivation Buster lacks, but will need to run the ranch successfully.

Buster returns from school

Meanwhile, Lily tries not to think about her own missed opportunities with regard to getting an education. She is therefore very surprised when she rides into town one day to pick up the mail and discovers a letter addressed to her from Mother Albertina. The nun still thinks that Lily should become a teacher, that she already knows enough to become one. She has written to tell Lily about a possible opportunity for her. The war in Europe has caused a shortage of teachers, especially in isolated places. Mother Albertina feels that if Lily can pass a government test being held in Santa Fe, she would probably be able to get a job as a teacher, even though she is only fifteen. Lily is, of course, very excited by this suggestion. Her parents, however, are unhappy about the idea. Her mother thinks it will be easier for her to get married if she remains at the ranch, as everyone in the valley knows her father is an important property owner. Her father has lots of reasons why she shouldn't go, but finally admits his main reason is that he needs her. But Lily knows the ranch will belong to Buster one day, and

An opportunity for Lily

Her parents are reluctant to let her take the test for teachers that she also needs to find her Purpose in life. This argument persuades Dad to at least let her take the test.

She passes the test and gets a job

Lily finds the test is not as difficult as she thought it would be, and she soon hears that she has passed. As a result, she is offered a job as an itinerant replacement teacher in Arizona. She is thrilled, and Dad accepts the situation: as fate has offered her this chance, she should take it. The school she is being sent to is five hundred miles away, and there is only one way for her to get there: on horseback. Lily works out that it will take her about four weeks to cover the distance, and that as long as Patches does not get injured, she will make it. Her mother fears for her safety, and her father gives her a gun, just in case she needs to defend herself. On the day she leaves, the whole family gets up to see her off and, after having breakfast, she sets off just after dawn.

III Promises

Promises

- Lily's first teaching job in Red Lake
- For four years, she teaches at various small schools, until there is no longer any work for her.
- Not wanting to return permanently to the KC Ranch, she moves to Chicago.
- Unable to find a teaching job in Chicago, she works as a maid.
- She makes a friend, Minnie, who is killed in a tragic accident.
- She falls in love and gets married; her husband turns out to be a bigamist, so she has the marriage annulled.

On the road to Red Lake

Lily and Patches travel to Red Lake, Arizona, on dirt tracks and old Indian trails. From time to time they pass other people, such as a cowboy or some Mexicans, but, although Lily always acknowledges them politely, she keeps contact to a minimum. They travel in the cool of the early morning, rest in the shade in the midday heat and then, when the day begins to cool down, they move on until darkness falls. They sleep outdoors every night. Whenever they come to one of the small towns along the way, Lily stops at the store to buy food and to ask advice about the next stretch of her journey. The storekeepers are happy to have someone to chat to, and tell her about the road ahead, draw her maps and advise her on the best places to camp for the night. Some of the places she passes through are so isolated that she might turn out to be the only customer the store has had all week.

Priscilla Loosefoot

Part of the journey passes by several Indian reservations, and one day Lily meets a half-Navajo woman, only a little bit older than she is, riding a donkey. Her name is Priscilla Loosefoot, and her mother gave her to a family of settlers in exchange for two mules. However, the family had treated her badly, so she'd run away and now survived by selling herbs she'd collected. The two young women travel together for the rest of the day, and camp together in the evening. Priscilla makes some Indian cakes for them to eat, and, unusually for a Navajo, talks a lot. She thinks that she and Lily would make a good team if they traveled together. During the night, Lily wakes up to find Priscilla searching her saddlebags. Immediately, Lily takes her gun out of her boot and points it at Priscilla, telling her that she has nothing of value. Priscilla admits that she had thought this was the case, but was checking anyway. She says that she and Lily could still make a good team if Lily is prepared to forget this incident: "Thing is, I don't get a lot of opportunities, and when one comes along, I gots to take it" (pg. 81). Although Lily understands this point of view, she knows she would now never be able to trust the other woman, and so orders her to stay where she is while she and Patches move on.

She reaches Red Lake after 28 days

By the time Lily reaches Red Lake, she has been traveling for 28 days. She is tired, dirty, thinner than when she set off and her skin has been darkened by the sun: "But I had made it, made it through that darned door" (pg. 82). She has taken the opportunity to make something of her life.

The town of Red Lake is situated around thirty miles to the south of the Grand Canyon, on a high plateau. Until recently, the land had mainly been used for grazing cattle, but now more farmers are moving into the area, hoping to grow crops there. The farmers have lots of children, and want them to get an education. The local school superintendent, Mr. MacIntosh, comes to explain the reason for the shortage of teachers in the area: many men had joined the army and gone to fight in the war. As a result, many women were moving to the towns to get a job in a factory, which paid well and were now vacant since the men had left. However, the education board still wants its teachers to have completed the eighth grade as a minimum qualification. As this was not the case for Lily, she is told that she will only be working at Red Lake until they find someone with better qualifications. Nevertheless, Mr. MacIntosh assures her that there will always be work for her in the area.

World War I is in progress and workers are leaving remote areas

The school at Red Lake consists of one room with a teacher's desk, benches for the children to sit on, and a blackboard, something that many schoolhouses did not have at the time. There is also an oil heater in the corner for the cold weather. However, there is no teacherage, i.e. a room for the teacher to live in, attached to the school, as can often be found in small schools in remote areas. Lily therefore sleeps on the floor. She has fifteen students to teach, many of them from very poor backgrounds, but their parents are all eager for them to learn. Lily is allowed to teach them whatever she wants, and finds that she loves her work. As the school has no books, the pupils bring books from home, anything they have, from the family Bible to seed catalogs, and Lily uses them as reading material. She finds that she is respected, is given gifts of food and receives invitations to dinner. She loves her job and is very happy.

The schoolhouse at Red Lake

Teaching materials

After several months, a qualified teacher is found for Red Lake, and Lily is sent to another town, Cow Springs. For three years, she teaches at a number of small, remote towns like these, never for more than a few months at a time. She is proud that she has taught so many children: it "made me feel like I was making a difference in their lives" (pg. 85). No matter what a child is like, she finds a way to teach him or her by finding out what he

She teaches in several different towns

or she is good at, and this gives her great satisfaction. It therefore comes as a shock when Mr. MacIntosh comes to tell her that, since the war is over, everyone is returning to their old jobs, and the school board no longer has any work for her. Although she understands that the soldiers returning after the war need jobs, she feels it is somewhat unfair that she is now not considered qualified for a job that she has been doing for four years. Mr. MacIntosh suggests that she will be able to marry one of the former soldiers, and then everything will be all right. Instead, Lily goes home to the KC Ranch.

No more work for Lily

Her first sighting of a plane

The most exciting part of Lily's journey home is when she sees an airplane for the first time in her life. Patches becomes nervous at the sound of the engine, but Lily manages to control her, and waves at the pilot as the plane passes. The pilot waves back, and Lily gallops after the plane, thrilled because, as someone who loves science, she suddenly understands how planes manage to stay in the air. It is the beginning of her fascination with airplanes.

Changes on the KC Ranch

Lily hasn't been home for four years, and when she gets back to the KC Ranch, she discovers that there have been some changes. A new wing has been built on to the side of the house, and flowers have been planted. Buster and Dorothy are married, and Dorothy is now in charge of the ranch, telling the rest of the family and the servants what needs to be done every day. Lily can tell that her parents are glad someone is there to run the ranch, as she once did, even though they complain that Dorothy is too bossy. Lily's sister Helen, who is now sixteen, is not much help around the place. She does not have much motivation and dislikes hard physical work, which will make it difficult for her to find a husband among the local ranch owners. Mom wants to send her to finishing school to improve her chances of getting a husband in the city, but Dorothy says they need to invest their money in the farm, not spend it on school. Helen's own ambition is to "become an actress" (pg. 89) in Los Angeles.

On Lily's first full day back at the ranch, Dad expects her to go out with him and work with the horses, as she always did. However, Lily has changed during the years she's been away. She no longer feels she belongs on the ranch, and is sure that she now wants a different kind of life. As well as this, she is convinced that motorized vehicles, such as cars and planes, will become more and more important, and that the days of carriages and carriage horses are numbered. Her father, however, does not believe cars will ever become popular and, as usual, starts complaining that things were better in the past and will be worse in the future. But Lily has become more objective with regard to her family while she's been away, and finds she does not agree with her father's opinions. Instead, she has come to realize that change is inevitable:

Her desire to break free

Horse-drawn carriages will soon be a thing of the past

> "What Dad didn't understand was that no matter how much he hated or feared the future, it was coming, and there was only one way to deal with it: by climbing aboard" (pg. 90).

She longs to discover more of the world, get a qualification, even learn to fly a plane. It becomes clear to her that she will never achieve any of these things by staying on the KC Ranch. Likewise, she is not prepared to wait around for a man to ask her to marry him. She wants to live in a place where she will have the opportunity to fulfill her ambitions, and that has to be a big city. This is why she decides to move to Chicago.

The train journey to Chicago takes four days, and is very exciting for Lily as she has never traveled by rail before. Chicago turns out to be completely different from anywhere she has ever been before. She's never seen so many people together in one place, or heard so much noise as the "ferocious din" (pg. 92) caused by the traffic and building work on the new skyscrapers that are being constructed around the city. The people seem different, too: they don't look into strangers' eyes and give them a friendly nod, as they do where Lily used to live, but simply ignore each other. She goes to see Lake Michigan and can hardly believe that so much water can be

Her first impressions of Chicago

contained in one place. She is used to living in places where every drop of water is precious, so precious that it frequently causes fights, where sometimes people are even killed because of the need for it.

Looking for work

Through a Catholic priest, Lily finds a respectable boardinghouse for women where she shares a room with three others. She immediately starts to look for a job, but this does not prove to be easy. Without qualifications, she has no chance of getting a teaching job. She has no experience of working in a shop, and all the jobs for clerks in companies are being taken by soldiers who have come back after the war. She comes to realize that the only jobs she has a chance of getting are as a factory worker or a maid. Working in a factory does not appeal to her; she feels that her chances of advancement would be better if she worked as a maid: she would have contact with people and might be able to persuade her employers to give her a better job if she played her cards right. Lily soon finds a job as a maid. It is hard work physically, but she is used to that and does not mind. However, she does mind the fact that her employer's wife has a very superior attitude towards her, although the woman, who she calls Mim, is actually rather stupid. Once, Lily even helps her with a crossword clue, which Mim does not like at all. She has been working there for two weeks when Mim comes to tell her that she is fired. Lily cannot understand why, as she has done an excellent job around the house. Mim's problem, however, is that "You don't seem to know your place" (pg 95). Lily looks at her directly, instead of looking down; Mim is obviously threatened by the fact that her maid is more intelligent than she is, and so Lily has to go.

She lacks the right attitude for a maid

It doesn't take Lily long to get another job. She has learnt her lesson and makes sure she doesn't step out of line, even though such humble behavior doesn't come naturally to her. In addition to this, she goes to evening classes in order to get her high-school diploma. Despite all the hard work, she loves living in Chicago as it is a lively, modern city. She also makes a friend called Minnie Hanagan, one of the girls she shares a room with at the boardinghouse. Minnie is a beautiful Irish girl,

Lily's friend Minnie

very self-confident, who talks a lot and has opinions about everything. Lily enjoys the chance to discuss the issues of the day with Minnie, especially since she has to keep quiet at work all day. The two girls go out on dates together, and have fun going to department stores to try on clothes, even though they cannot afford them. Unlike Lily, Minnie is not intimidated by superior shop assistants, and does not allow anyone to treat her badly. For Lily, she was "the closest thing I'd ever had to a genuine friend" (pg. 95). One evening, Lily returns to the boardinghouse to hear the news that Minnie has been killed in an accident at work. She worked in a beer-bottling factory, and her long hair, which she was supposed to tie back at work, had got caught up in the machinery and pulled her in there, too. During and after her funeral, Lily reflects on how quickly and unexpectedly someone's life can end. In the evening, after the funeral, she takes a pair of scissors and symbolically cuts off her own long hair.

Minnie's accident and death

Lily cuts her hair

At the time, in the 1920s, it is very modern for women to have short hair: it gives them freedom from caring for long hair and is safer in a world that is becoming more industrialized. Lily also finds that she attracts more attention from men with her new haircut. One man seems particularly interested in her, and speaks to her when she is walking along by the lake one day. He introduces himself as Ted Conover, a vacuum-cleaner salesman. Although Lily realizes right from the start that he is "a bit of a huckster" (pg. 98), she can't help liking him. He is cheerful, talkative and makes her laugh. She falls in love with him, although she feels this might partly be because she is lonely and vulnerable after Minnie's death. After their first meeting, Lily and Ted start dating, although his salesman job often takes him out of town for several days. They go to baseball games, boxing matches and he teaches her to swim. Ted proposes to her six weeks after they first meet, with a diamond engagement ring. Lily accepts and their wedding is held in the Catholic Church where she asked for advice on where to live when she first arrived in the city. The newly-weds are not able to go away on honeymoon, but they move into a boardinghouse for married couples and drink a bottle

She meets Ted Conover

Lily and Ted get married

of gin to celebrate their wedding day. The following day, they both return to work.

She likes being married

A little to her surprise, Lily enjoys married life: it is the first time she has really shared her life with another person. Ted has a lot of plans for the future, and encourages Lily in her ambitions to get a diploma and go to college. He makes her believe she can do anything she sets her mind to. They decide not to have any children at this point in time, but to save as much money as they can so that they will be able to turn their dreams into reality. Ted works away from Chicago a lot, and Lily completes her high-school diploma at night school. One day, on her way back from shopping for her employers, Lily is hit by a car. As she knows how to fall from her horse-breaking days, she is not badly hurt, but the driver of the car, who she refers to as "Slick" because of his slicked-back hair, insists on taking her to hospital to make sure she is really all right. At the hospital, Slick says she should call Ted to let him know what has happened, and, when he hears that her husband is traveling on business, suggests calling his office, as they will be able to contact him. However, when she calls his office and tells them what she wants, she gets a terrible shock: "Ted ain't on the road. He just left for lunch. And his wife's name's Margaret" (pg. 104).

She is involved in a traffic accident

Lily needs to find out the truth about Ted

On hearing this, Lily runs out of the hospital, trying to calm down. She feels the immediate need to find out the truth about Ted. She therefore waits opposite his office at the end of the working day, and sees her husband leaving the building with the other workers. Clearly he is not working away from Chicago after all. She follows him onto the El, then to a run-down part of town where he goes into an apartment block. There are no names on any of the mailboxes, but she manages to get into the building and listens at every door until she hears his voice. She knocks, and the door is answered by a woman carrying a young child. Lily asks her if she is Margaret, Ted Conover's wife. When asked who she is, Lily nearly tells her, but in the end cannot bear to hurt the other woman. Instead, she pretends she is from the census office, and discovers that Ted lives there with Margaret and three children. Lily leaves without revealing anything about herself.

On her way home, Lily is struck by another terrible thought: what may have happened to her and Ted's joint bank account, in which they had managed to save nearly two hundred dollars. First thing the next morning, she goes to the bank and discovers that there are now only ten dollars in the account. She returns to the boardinghouse to get her revolver and travels to Ted's office. When she sees him sitting with his colleague with his feet on the table, smoking and reading the paper, she becomes so furious that she starts screaming abuse at him: "You no-good low-down dirty lying scum-sucking son of a bitch!" (pg. 107). She hits him several times with her bag, which is heavy because the revolver is inside. The other man leaves quickly, and Lily demands some answers about why Ted has been lying to her and why all their money is gone. At first he remains hostile towards her, but gradually breaks down and admits he took their money because he owed it to gamblers, but had meant to pay it back. As far as Margaret is concerned, he claims that it is Lily he really loves, not the mother of his children, and he had only lied to her so that he could be with her. He tells her he is sure his love for her has ruined her life. Lily, however, has nothing but contempt for Ted, and certainly feels no sympathy for him, as he seems to expect: "You have a mighty high opinion of yourself," I told him. "The fact is, you don't love me, and you haven't destroyed me. You don't have what it takes to do that" (pg. 108). With that, she leaves.

Ted has taken most of the money they saved

Lily confronts Ted

She rejects her husband and his excuses

Although Lily is shocked by what has happened, she knows she will survive. She feels that her current situation is similar in some ways to Minnie's death: a sudden disaster can change things in an instant. In her case, she realizes that the whole thing started with her accident: if the car had not hit her, she would not have found out about Ted and would have gone on as before. She herself has not been killed, but the life she thought she had no longer exists. Chicago has not been a lucky place for her, and she knows it is time for her to go home. Before she does so, she goes to see the priest and explains her situ-

Someone's life can be turned upside-down in a moment

She decides to leave Chicago

She applies to have her marriage annulled

ation to him. She finds out that she can apply to have her marriage annulled if she can provide evidence that her husband was already married. She manages to get a copy of Ted's first marriage certificate, and the priest promises to send in the application for her. Lily is also concerned about Margaret, Ted's wife, feeling she should know the truth. She therefore writes a letter to the other woman, but decides not to take any legal action against Ted, mainly for the sake of his family. Her final act is to take her diamond engagement ring to a jeweler's, meaning to sell it and put the money towards her further education, maybe even buy herself something special with it. However, the jeweler informs her that the ring is a worthless fake, so she throws it into the lake.

Plans for the future

After this, Lily knows she needs to focus on her future, and is determined to study for a teaching qualification. She applies for a place at the teacher's college in Flagstaff, Arizona, and works very hard at three different jobs, saving nearly everything she earns so that she can pay for her tuition. By the time her marriage annulment is approved, she has saved enough to pay for the first year of college. The day she leaves Chicago, she has very few material possessions, but knows that she is taking a lot away with her in the form of experience, especially with regard to trusting people. As the train pulls away from the city, she realizes that nobody will miss her and that, although she has now got her high-school diploma, all the work she has done for other people has been a waste of time – she has got nothing out of it. She thinks back to her time as a teacher in the remote southern towns and knows that what she really wants is to feel needed again, as she did back then.

She wants to be needed

IV The Red Silk Shirt

→ Lily goes to college in Flagstaff to get a teaching qualification. → She is offered the chance to work as a teacher in Red Lake again. → She becomes friendly with some of the local characters, such as Rooster and Big Jim Smith. → She gets a letter from her sister Helen, who has become accidentally pregnant and urgently needs her help. → Helen commits suicide.	The Red Silk Shirt

Back home at the KC Ranch, Lily finds that not much has changed. Buster and Dorothy now have a couple of children, and have complete responsibility for the running of the farm. Mom has become more delicate, and Helen has gone to live in Los Angeles. She has not yet managed to get a part in a movie, but has met some producers and is working in a hat shop. Lily wonders how Helen is really coping in LA, but their mother, in her desire to find a good husband for her daughters, was keen for her to go. Mom is less certain about Lily's chances of finding a good husband now that she's already been married once. She is glad that Lily is going to college so that she will have a back-up plan if she doesn't manage to get married again. Patches the horse is also still there, getting on in years now, but Lily is still able to ride her, and enjoys doing so after her time in Chicago when she'd had no opportunity to go riding.

Dorothy and Buster now run the ranch

Mom wonders how Lily will get a husband now

This time around, nobody expects her to stay on the ranch. Lily is glad, as she no longer feels she belongs there, and is happy to leave for Flagstaff as soon as she can. She loves studying at college and makes the most of her time there, working hard to achieve her goal. However, she has only saved up enough money for the first year's tuition and does not know how she will pay for the rest. This problem is solved for her in an unexpected way. After only one semester, the president of the college tells her that the town of Red Lake is looking for a teacher and still remembers her. If she wants the job, it is hers, even though she hasn't finished college. The col-

She does not belong on the ranch any more

She is offered a teaching job back in Red Lake

lege president thinks it will be hard for her to decide, as it would probably be difficult for her to complete her college degree if she leaves now. Lily sees it differently: "It didn't seem a tough choice at all. I could either pay money to go to classes or get paid for teaching classes. 'When do I start?' I asked" (pg. 117).

Lily returns to Red Lake

Once again, Lily makes the journey to Red Lake on Patches. There are more people on the road now, and there are even cars from time to time, but Red Lake is still a remote place and a lot of the time she travels without seeing anyone else. The character of the town, however, has changed since she was last there, with more "scoundrels and eccentrics" (pg 118) living there. In addition to this, there are more farms and shops than before; there is even a garage and a gasoline pump to deal with the increase in cars. A teacherage has been added on to the schoolhouse, which means Lily has a place to live with some privacy. She now has thirty-six children to teach; she makes sure they speak to her respectfully and does not accept any rudeness.

Lily breaks the mustang

She impresses the men with her riding skills

When she goes to collect her first paycheck, Lily has an experience that improves her status in the town. She has to collect her money from the town hall, next to which there is an enclosure containing a small wild horse: she can tell at a glance that it is a bad-tempered animal. There are two deputies inside the town hall, who, when they find out who Lily is and why she has come, decide to have some fun with her first. They are under the impression that Lily is a teacher from the big city, who thinks she is superior to them. One of them, who she refers to as Rooster because he is "a skinny guy with rooster legs and close-set eyes" (pg. 120), tells her that she has to ride the mustang before she can have her paycheck. Of course, Lily knows she will be able to do so, but pretends to be a gentle city girl without much experience of riding. The men can hardly stop themselves laughing, being so sure that she will immediately be thrown from the horse. However, Lily sees that the mustang is "just another half-broke horse" (pg. 121) and she knows how to deal with him. She manages to ride the horse without too much difficulty, which wipes the smile off the face of the two deputies – in fact they seem slightly shocked by what they have just witnessed. It is clear to Lily that the men must have tried to tame the horse themselves, and failed, and can therefore hardly believe that she has managed to do so.

The deputies misjudge Lily

Before long, the inhabitants of Red Lake get to hear about Lily and the mustang, which gains her a great deal of respect. Not only do people now ask her advice, both on horses and children with whom they are having problems, but Rooster becomes her "faithful sidekick" (pg. 122), a friend and supporter. Rooster is not only a deputy, but makes some extra cash by doing various jobs around the town, mostly to do with horses. Lily comes to like him, and starts spending her free time with him, playing poker on a Saturday night with him and his friends, drinking whiskey (even though this is the time of Prohibition, and is therefore illegal). She usually wins at poker, even if only small amounts. Rooster also owns the mustang, whose name is Red Devil, that Lily broke, and she rides it for him in local horse races, often winning there, too. She describes her status in the town at this point in her life:

She gains a position of respect in the town

She begins horse-racing again

> "I became known as Lily Casey, the mustang-breaking, poker-playing, horse-race-winning schoolmarm of Coconino County, and it wasn't half bad to be in a place where no one had a problem with a woman having a moniker like that" (pg. 123).

Lily soon realizes that Rooster is falling in love with her, but she tells him that she's got one failed marriage behind her and does not intend to remarry. She thinks he has accepted this, so is surprised when he comes to the teacherage one day to ask her something, clearly embarrassed by what he is going to say. However, it turns out that he is illiterate, and wants Lily to teach him to read and write. So he comes to the schoolhouse on Saturday afternoons for lessons, and then the two of them go out for the evening to play cards. At this time, Lily is still taking part in horse races with Red Devil, which she often wins. She uses some of the money she has won to buy herself a red silk shirt, which she then wears in every race, making herself instantly recognizable to the

Lily teaches Rooster to read

Her red silk shirt

spectators. She is proud of the fact that the shirt has obviously been bought from a mail-order catalog rather than being home-made, making her stand out from the rest: "that shirt became my trademark" (pg. 124).

That spring, Lily and Rooster go to take part in a race meet, bigger and more professional than the ones they are used to. During the second heat, a car backfires as she is passing on Red Devil, who bucks, throwing her off his back. Lily puts her hands over her head and lies still until the other horses have passed by, then gets up, gets back on Red Devil and makes him finish the race, even though there is now no chance of them winning. This gains her the respect of the judge, who raises his hat to her, and later comes over to talk to her. Rooster knows him, and introduces him as Jim Smith, also known as Big Jim, the owner of the town's new garage. He is "a big man with a deliberate way of moving, a weathered face, and steady pale blue eyes" (pg. 125). Lily is still angry about the car backfiring, as she is sure she would have won the race if that hadn't happened. This makes Big Jim think that she doesn't like cars, but she admits to him that she would like to learn to drive. Big Jim offers to teach her.

Lily's first meeting with Big Jim

Lily is happy to take Jim up on his offer, and learns to drive his Model T Ford. It is very difficult to start the car, but once the engine is running, she finds driving very easy and a lot of fun, too: "a hoot" (pg. 126). In fact, Lily comes to love cars more than horses, and finds they have many advantages over the latter, such as not needing food or running away.

She learns to drive

> "They also didn't buck, bite or rear, and they didn't need to be broke and trained, or caught and saddled up every time you needed to go somewhere. They didn't have a mind of their own. Cars obeyed you" (pg. 126).

Before long, she is speeding around the town, and soon she and Jim start taking trips to the Grand Canyon, going on picnics and riding horses together. Although he hasn't said anything to her, Lily realizes that Jim is courting her. She likes him and sees several advantages that he has in comparison to her ex-husband, but does not want to get married again. Jim had been born a Mormon, but was not a practicing one. His father, Lot Smith, had been a leading figure in the Mormon Church, with eight wives and fifty-two children. His children were encouraged to become independent and do things for themselves, as a result of which Jim was already excellent at shooting and dealing with horses when he was just fourteen. He had worked in Canada, as a homesteader in Arizona, and fought in Siberia during the First World War. By now he was nearly fifty, twenty years older than Lily, but still able to do lots of hard physical work. He had excellent eyesight and was extremely observant. Moreover, he never got angry; "he was dependable and established" (pg. 129), running an honest business. Lily enjoys being with him, but the question of marriage is not raised between them.

Jim's background

One day, Lily gets a letter from her sister Helen. Helen is still in Hollywood, and has not yet managed to realize her ambition to become a movie star, although in her previous letters she has always told Lily that her big break is likely to come at any time. In these letters, she also talks about the latest "Mr. Wonderful" (pg. 130) in her life who is going to help her fulfill her dreams and maybe even marry her. However, none of these men seem to be around for very long, and Lily has the impression they are just using her sister:

A letter from Helen

> "I wrote her letters warning her not to count on men to take care of her and to come up with a fallback plan in case, as seemed pretty obvious by now, the movie career didn't pan out" (ibid.).

But Helen ignores her advice, telling her this is the way things get done in Hollywood. And now she is pregnant, and her boyfriend has disowned her because she did not want to have a backstreet abortion. She is now desperate, knowing that she will lose her job in the milliner's and will no longer be able to go to movie auditions once it becomes obvious that she is pregnant. She does not want to return to her parents' ranch and is now thinking about whether to have the abortion after all. Lily wants to prevent this, fearing that her sister could die during such an operation, and instead thinks she should

Helen's pregnancy

have the baby, first coming to stay with her at Red Lake to have time to think about her options.

Helen comes to stay with Lily

When Lily goes to meet her sister from the train in Flagstaff, she notices at once how thin Helen has become. She has dyed her hair, has obviously been crying, and needs a cigarette as soon as she gets into the car. Practical as ever, Lily has a list of possible plans for Helen. She could write to their parents and explain the situation, as she is convinced they would still let Helen come home, despite what has happened. Helen could give the baby up for adoption, or perhaps marry a local man – there were sure to be some who would take her on, even in her condition. Helen, however, does not seem to be able to concentrate on the reality of her situation, seeming more worried about whether giving birth would ruin her figure and spoil her chances of getting a movie role. Her attitude is a complete contrast to Lily's, but Lily is sure she will be able to help her sister, given time.

Helen moves into the teacherage with Lily, who gives her plenty of reassurance that everything will be all right. Even with rest and support, however, Helen does not seem able to make a decision, which starts to annoy Lily after a while:

> "I'd hoped that once she'd gotten some rest, her mind would clear, and she'd be able to start thinking about her future in a constructive fashion. But she continued to be vague and listless, talking about Hollywood in a dreamy way that, quite frankly, irritated me" (pg. 133).

Helen has to decide what to do about the baby

Hoping that fresh air will help, she takes Helen out on walks around the town, and to horse races. Jim Smith, who Lily has seen as a possible husband for Helen, is clearly not the right man for her after all. Rooster likes her, but he does not appeal to Helen. What she does like is Lily's red shirt, and trying it on seems to cheer her up. The problem is that her pregnancy is now starting to show and they will very soon have to make a decision, because "her problems weren't going to go away" (pg. 134).

Lily and Helen go to services at the local Catholic Church. The priest, Father Cavanaugh, is unpleasant and unfriendly, but Lily hopes Helen might meet a man there. One day, the air is so stuffy that Helen faints. Father Cavanaugh hurries to her side, and discovers that she is pregnant, and clearly unmarried as she is not wearing a wedding ring. He announces this in front of his congregation, which means that before long the whole town knows about it. The priest makes her confess her sins and tries to force her to go to a home for sinful women like herself, but Helen refuses. From that day forwards, the people in the town start to look at the two sisters in a different way. Women ignore them and cowboys look at them as if they are the type to sleep around. Then Lily has a visit from Superindentent MacIntosh, who informs her that the Arizona Board of Education has received several complaints from parents about the fact that there is an unmarried, pregnant woman living in the teacherage, and that it is having a bad influence on the students. If Helen does not leave, Lily will lose her job. Lily can hardly believe what she is hearing, and is angry about the double standards that the townspeople seem to have:

The town finds out that Helen is pregnant

Lily will lose her job if Helen stays

> "The parents of my schoolkids included cattle rustlers, drunks, land speculators, bootleggers, gamblers, and former prostitutes. They didn't mind me racing horses, playing poker or drinking contraband whiskey, but my showing some compassion to a sister who'd been taken advantage of and then abandoned by a smooth-talking scoundrel filled them with moral indignation. It made me want to throttle them all" (pg. 136 f.).

It does not help that Helen has overheard everything. Lily is still sure that everything will be all right. Her plan is to send her sister back home to the KC Ranch and stay there until the baby is born. She will earn money for Helen and the baby by horse-racing. Once the baby is born, Buster and Dorothy can bring it up and Helen can move away again. Helen does not believe that her parents will welcome her, but that instead they will be ashamed of her and not allow her to stay with them. She feels that she is not able to cope any more, because she is not a strong person like Lily: "Don't you ever feel like

She is sure the family will help Helen

Lily's plans for her sister's future

giving up? […] I just feel like giving up" (pg. 138). Lily tries to make her see things positively, reminding her how they escaped from the flood when they were children, and how she found a way to get an education and a profession even though she had to leave school. Thinking she has finally managed to comfort her sister, Lily feels a lot better, and even plans an outing to the Grand Canyon as a special treat. It is a beautiful November morning, and Lily goes to borrow Jim's car while Helen gets ready. Suddenly, she feels as if she is being strangled and has a premonition that something is very wrong. She runs back to the schoolhouse as fast as she can, but she is too late: Helen has hanged herself.

Helen commits suicide

Because suicide is considered a mortal sin by the Catholic Church, Father Cavanaugh refuses have Helen buried in the Catholic cemetery. Instead, Lily drives out of town with Jim and Rooster until they find a beautiful place in the countryside, looking down on a valley full of trees: "so beautiful that I knew in God's eyes it must be sacred" (pg. 141). It is here that they bury Helen, wearing Lily's red silk shirt.

V Lambs

Lambs	
	➞ Helen's death makes Lily long for a baby of her own. ➞ She asks Jim Smith to marry her. ➞ She gives up teaching, moves to a new town and goes to work with Jim at his garage. ➞ Lily and Jim have two children. ➞ Hard economic times threaten their business, so Lily sells bootleg alcohol until it becomes too dangerous to do so. ➞ Jim impresses local ranchers by sorting out a problem with some lambs. ➞ Jim's business goes bankrupt, but he and Lily are offered the chance to run a ranch that is owned by Poms. ➞ Jim and Lily improve the ranch by having dams built to conserve water during the few times that it rains in that region. ➞ They save the main dam during a severe flood, thereby saving the ranch.

In the months following Helen's suicide, Lily feels very unhappy and depressed: "When people kill themselves, they think they're ending the pain, but all they're doing is passing it on to those they leave behind" (pg. 145). Her job is the only reason she has for getting up in the mornings, but she can no longer see any point in all the other activities she used to enjoy, such as horse riding or going for a drive. She decides to give up her job, although she is not able to do so immediately because of her contract. She knows the children should not be held responsible for their parents' actions, but she has had enough of the town of Red Lake and plans to leave at the end of the school year. She has even become disillusioned with teaching, feeling that she has given the children so much and got nothing in return from their families. In addition to this, the fact that Helen was pregnant when she died has made Lily think about having a child of her own. Gradually, this idea helps her get over the pain of her loss, and she comes to realize that she wants to act on it.

Lily plans to quit her teaching job

She wants to have a baby

To maintain her respectability, Lily will of course need a husband before she can have a baby, which is what makes her turn to Jim Smith. She knows that he is the right man for her: "He had plenty of good qualities, but the most important one was that I felt I could trust that man inside and out" (pg. 146). Her decision is made, and without further ado she goes to Jim's garage and asks him to marry her. He does not even need to think about it: "Lily Casey, I wanted to marry you ever since I saw you take that fall off that mustang and then get right back on him" (pg. 146). Lily has two conditions, however: they must agree to be equal partners in everything they do as a married couple, and Jim must promise not to marry any additional wives (which, as a Mormon, he could do). It is easy for Jim to promise that: "from what I know of you, you're just about as much woman as any man can handle" (pg. 146).

She decides to marry Jim

In Lily's second marriage, everything is different right from the start. Jim buys her a real engagement ring, they get married in her classroom rather than a church, and Jim will do anything for her. Because she wants to

They move to the town of Ash Fork

leave Red Lake, he moves his garage to Ash Fork, a busy town about thirty miles away. Lily and Jim build their new garage themselves, and before long their business is doing well. Lily takes an active part in the day-to-day running of the garage, doing jobs just as pumping gas and changing flat tires. By this time, Lily is already twenty-nine, which is comparatively old to be starting a family, but she is looking forward to doing so and is soon expecting her first baby. As well as the garage, they build a small house for themselves on Route 66, no more than a dusty dirt road at the time. They buy themselves a plumbing system from the Sears catalog and install it in the house: they have running water in the kitchen and a flush toilet, both of which fill Lily with such an immense sense of pride that she always offers visitors a glass of tap water or use of the toilet.

Lily's first child

Their house in Ash Fork

As Lily reaches the end of her pregnancy, Jim starts to become worried that it might not be good for her to work at the garage. Lily, however, is used to working all the time and does not cope well with being at home all day. Therefore she goes back to work at the garage until just before the baby is born. When the time comes, Lily has her baby at home with the help of Granny Combs, a local midwife who is an expert in childbirth despite being somewhat eccentric. All goes well and Lily gives birth to a girl, who she names Rosemary. After the birth, Granny Combs lays out the Tarot cards to look into the baby's future. Apparently the little girl will have a "long" and "eventful" life, and will be "a wanderer" (pg. 152). These predictions later turn out to be true. Rosemary is a beautiful baby who reminds Lily of Helen; because, in her opinion, Helen's beauty had been a curse rather than a blessing, Lily decides that she will never tell her daughter how good-looking she is.

Their daughter Rosemary is born

Lily and Jim's son is born one and a half years later, this time in the new hospital forty miles from where they live. In fact, their son is the first child to be born there. Named after his father, the boy is always known as Little Jim. This is the time when northern Arizona begins to be affected by an economic crisis. One factor is that the land had been over-farmed, especially by farmers and

Their son Little Jim is born

ranchers from the east of the USA who did not know how thin the topsoil was, and had therefore over-grazed and over-plowed it, destroying what little good farmland there was. In addition to this, the rest of the country is suffering from the Great Depression, which now starts to have a knock-on effect in their part of the country. For example, many people in the big cities can no longer afford to eat beef, which in turn affects the cattle market, making some of the ranches in Arizona bankrupt. Many people who used to work on these ranches leave the area, headed for California in the hope of finding work there. In turn, Jim and Lily's business is affected, as many people no longer have enough money for gasoline and are forced to sell their cars and tractors. Moreover, Jim often lets people pay less than the full amount and repairs their vehicles free of charge.

The Depression reaches Arizona

The bad times hit Jim's business

Lily goes through their finances and sees that they too will soon be bankrupt if things continue like this, especially since they have loans to pay back. She wonders what they can do to make some extra money. Then Mr. Lee, a Chinese man who makes a lot of money selling his food from a tent in the town, comes to see them. He has a sideline to his business, selling illegal alcohol to his customers, and has now discovered that the revenuers are on his track. He needs somewhere to hide his liquor. He and Jim get on well because they fought under similar conditions during the war, and they trust each other. This is why Jim allows Mr. Lee to hide his cases of drink under Little Jim's crib. Thinking about this, Lily comes up with a plan. She could sell bootleg alcohol at their back door to make a bit of extra cash. It would be carrying on a family tradition, as her grandfather had sold drink from the KC Ranch, and, unlike her father, she does not think drinking is necessarily a bad thing:

Lily decides to sell bootleg alcohol

> "I never saw anything wrong with an honest man taking a well-deserved drink. I even had one myself from time to time" (pg. 156).

Jim is not convinced that this is a good idea: he is afraid that Lily might get caught and end up in prison. However, Lily is sure being a mother of two and a respected schoolteacher is the perfect cover for this kind of operation. They would be doing a service for hardworking people with little money, they would have no expenses, and it was the only way she can think of to earn enough extra money to stop them from going bankrupt. After a while, Jim agrees, although he is unhappy about it. Mr. Lee agrees to give her two cases of drink per month as long as she shares the profits with him.

The sale of illegal drink saves their business

It doesn't take long for Lily to make a success of her new sideline. She will only sell drink to people she knows or who are recommended to her, she does not give anyone credit or sell to anyone who seems to be using money they needed for something else, such as rent, to buy alcohol. Before long, she is making about twenty dollars a month, which is enough to keep them afloat financially.

The Camel brothers' sheep are brought to town

Chaos when the lambs and ewes are separated

In spring, Jim has the chance to show how skilled he is in dealing with animals. The owners of a nearby ranch, the Camel brothers, have their large flock of sheep brought to town, as the animals are going to be sold. The sheep make a huge noise as they are driven to the shipping station; once they are there, one of the ranch hands decides to separate the lambs from the ewes. They quickly come to see that this is a huge mistake: the lambs are hungry and need their mothers to feed, while the mothers are distressed because they can no longer find their babies. So the ranch hands open the gate again to let the lambs find their mothers. However, because there are so many of them, this just makes the situation much worse. The lambs become even more hungry and weak in their desperate search for their mothers, and the ewes will not let any strange lambs feed from them, as they want to keep their milk for their own lambs. By now, a lot of the townspeople have come to watch, including Lily, Rosemary and Little Jim, and by the time the Camel brothers arrive the situation has got out of hand. They have no idea what to do, so Lily suggests that they ask Jim for advice.
Jim immediately realizes what has to be done: the ewes have to be tricked into accepting strange lambs, allowing the lambs to drink before they die of hunger. Once the lambs have been saved, the ewes can be reunited with their own lambs. To do this, he has Lily fetch an old

sheet while he gets some kerosene. The sheet is torn into small pieces, dipped in kerosene and wiped on the ewes' noses. This stops the ewes from being able to smell the lambs, and therefore they do not know if the lamb feeding from them is theirs or not. The lambs are able to drink the milk they so urgently need and their lives are saved. After this, Jim gets the ranch hands to separate the lambs from the ewes again, and then bring the lambs into the pen with the mother sheep one at a time, carrying each one around until it has found its mother. Because there are so many sheep, this procedure takes nearly two days, including time feeding the unclaimed lambs in the same way as before. Rosemary, who is three years old, is fascinated and worried at the same time in case any of the lambs do not manage to find their mothers. In the end, they discover one lamb that none of the ewes wanted; the Camel brothers give it to Jim, who lets Rosemary keep it as a pet. Named Mei-Mei, Chinese for "little sister" (pg. 161), the animal follows Rosemary around wherever she goes.

Jim saves the lambs

Rosemary gets to keep a lamb as a pet

Not long after this event, a man comes to the house to buy some bootleg. Just by looking at him, Lily can tell that he's already had too much to drink. The man's car is parked outside the house, and a woman and a girl are waiting in it. He is clearly used to getting what he wants, but Lily notices that the two passengers in his car are not looking happy. She therefore refuses to sell him any drink, which makes him very angry:

Lily refuses to sell alcohol to a drunk

> "... when he realized I wasn't giving in and he'd be leaving empty-handed, he really lost it, telling me I was going to regret crossing him and calling me nothing but the sister of a whore who'd hanged herself" (pg. 161).

This is the last straw for Lily. Telling the man to wait, she goes to get her pistol and points it directly at him. She isn't going to shoot him, she tells him, because of the women, but he should leave and never return.

When Lily tells Jim about the incident, he is sure that the matter will not end there. It therefore comes as no great surprise when they are visited by two men in uniform a couple of days later. They enter the house and

A visit from two deputies

tell Lily they have come to investigate a report of the illegal sale of alcohol from her house. Although they do not know it, the alcohol is in the very same room as they are, hidden under the baby's crib. Rosemary suddenly runs into the room, sees the men and starts screaming. This in turn makes her lamb bleat and wakes up Little Jim. Lily takes advantage of the chaos:

> "'Does this look like a speakeasy?'" I asked. 'I'm a schoolteacher! I'm a mother! I got my hands full here just taking care of these kids'" (pg. 163).

This and all the noise seems to convince the lawmen she is telling the truth, and they leave without investigating any further. Later, when Jim comes home, both he and Lily are able to see the funny side of the men's visit, but Jim is now convinced that they must stop selling bootleg liquor before they get caught. They do so, and go bankrupt six months later.

Lily stops selling bootleg

As they seem to have no future in Ash Fork, Lily and Jim decide to sell most of the contents of their garage and try their luck in California. However, they then receive an interesting offer. Blackie Camel, one of the owners of the lambs Jim had saved, has become friends with Jim since the incident. He tells them that his ranch has been sold to an English investment group, who want to use it as a cattle farm. The investors asked him if he knows of anyone who could run the ranch, and Blackie thought Jim would be ideal for the job. Jim and Lily immediately realize that they must seize this opportunity, but say they will think about it, not wanting to admit that they are desperate. A few days later, Jim is offered the job. Instead of selling their possessions, they load everything onto a carriage, and, with Rooster's help, make the journey to Seligman, the closest town to the new ranch. From there they have to travel a further fifteen miles along Route 66, then nine miles along a dirt track. After a day's travel, they arrive at the gate of the ranch. The ranch is large: it is another four miles from the gate to the ranch buildings. The area is vast and empty:

An offer to run a ranch

Lily and her family move to the ranch near Seligman

> "From where we stood, you could see to forever, and there wasn't a single other house, human being, or the slightest sign of civilization, only the huge sky, the endless grassy plain, and the distant mountains" (pg. 167).

There is only one ranch hand left, as all the rest have been fired. His name is Old Jake, "a grizzled, stogie-chewing coot who came limping out of the barn to greet us" (ibid.). The reason for his limp is that he put his foot on a railway track so that it would get run over by a train – this injury meant he did not have to fight in the First World War. He shows them around the property: the ranch is well-equipped with tools, there is a garage with a number of carriages, wagons and cars, and a corral with some ponies. Jim and Lily can see that, although the ranch is not luxurious, the buildings are sturdy and they have everything they need. They are sure that they'll be able to do a good job of running the ranch, even though it will be very hard work:

Old Jake

> "We were too far from town to count on anyone else for anything. Jim and I would have to be our own veterinarian, farrier, mechanic, butcher, cook, as well as cattle driver, ranch manager, husband and wife, and mother and father of two little children" (pg. 169).

Running the ranch will not be easy as they will have to do everything themselves

But the two of them are not afraid of hard work and are aware that they are lucky to have been given an opportunity like this.

On their first morning at the ranch, Jim tells them that they need to take a tour of the whole property. As it covers an area of nearly 160 square miles, they realize it will take them a week to reach the outer fence on horseback. They take one pony to carry supplies of food and other necessary items, Jim and Old Jake ride a pony each, and Lily goes on Patches. The children ride with their parents. They discover the main problem with the land: in the course of their ten-day trip, they do not once see a natural source of water. The land is completely dry. Once they have completed their tour, Jim has a water witch come out to test the land for a water supply, but none can be found. Lily realizes that their only possible source of water is rain, and that they need to find a way to trap rainwater during the flash floods that would come a few times a year. She tells Jim that they should build a dam, and has an idea about how they could do so: they could rent a bulldozer. She finds a company that would rent them one, and she and Jim decide to talk to

Exploring the ranch

The need for water

some of the English investors who will soon be coming out to meet them.

The Poms

The Englishmen, or Poms, are of course very different from the ranch dwellers, but they are aware that they know nothing about ranching and are happy for Jim and Lily to run the place their way. To give the Poms a taste of ranch life, they cook beef for them on an open fire and Lily prepares some delicacies such as rattlesnake stew. After the meal, Jim explains to them how essential water is in this area and tells them of the plan to build a dam. Having a reliable water supply would mean they could raise as many as twenty thousand cattle, increasing the profit the ranch made as more could be sold. The Poms agree to pay for the bulldozer, which soon arrives, and becomes an attraction for local people who have never seen anything like it. They have dams built on various different parts of the ranch, and when the rain comes it fills up the ponds they have dug out. The largest one is in front of their ranch house, and Jim is very proud of it. In summer, people come from far away to swim in it and they allow their neighbors to have some of the water if they need it. It is soon known as "Big Jim's Dam", and then just as "Big Jim" (pg. 176).

Big Jim's Dam

Officially, the ranch is called the Arizona Incorporated Cattle Ranch; Lily and Jim refer to it as the AIC or The Ranch rather than call it something more romantic: "A fancy name, Jim liked to say, was a sure sign that the owner didn't know the first thing about ranching" (pg. 177). Those were the kind of people who had gone bankrupt during the Depression, in addition to people who did know what they were doing but had been unlucky. These bankruptcies mean that Jim is able to buy plenty of cattle very cheaply. He also hires some cowboys to help him with the work, most of whom are either Mexican or from the Havasupai tribe. They are generally young men who have suffered abuse at home and run away, becoming a cowboy as it was one of the very few alternatives they had. They are skilled at "sticking" horses, i.e. being able to stay in the saddle on the back of a mustang. They would get wild horses from the open countryside and take them to the corral, where they

The cowboys on The Ranch

would partly break them. Although the cowboys often get thrown from these mustangs, they never give up: "They weren't much more than half-broke horses themselves" (pg. 177). Rosemary, watching the procedure with her mother, thinks that the horses want to be free rather than be forced to work for people. Lily is as pragmatic as ever: "In this life [...] hardly anyone gets to do what they want to do" (pg. 178).

Young cowboys as half-broke horses

Working on horseback, the cowboys round up the cattle to be branded. All of the young men live in the bunkhouse, an outbuilding on the ranch, and Lily cooks for them. Rosemary is not allowed to go near the bunkhouse or the men, but she herself is "also a little like a half-broke horse" (ibid.). She runs wild on the ranch and enjoys riding out with her father. She is fearless when it comes to animals of all kinds and wants them all to be able to run free. One day, however, she is forced to learn a hard lesson. The English investors have sent Jim a purebreed Guernsey cow to thank him for his work on the ranch. The cow, who they have named Bossie, gives especially rich milk with cream, and Lily plans to breed from her, selling the calf and saving the money for the future. But one day the door to Bossie's stall is left open. The cow escapes to the granary, where she eats so much feed that she dies, despite Jim and Old Jake's efforts to save her. Rosemary is distraught about the cow's death, although she claims it was her brother who let Bossie out, and Lily is furious. Since she cannot prove who is responsible, she cannot punish either child, but she gives her daughter this warning:

Rosemary is compared to a half-broke horse

Bossie the cow

> "Just you remember [...] that this is what could happen when an animal gets freedom. Animals act like they hate to be penned up, but the fact is, they don't know what to do with freedom. And a lot of times it kills them" (pg. 180).

Animals cannot always be free

The family settles in well to life on the ranch. Because of the huge amount of work that needs to be done, Lily keeps things as basic as possible: she only cleans the house from time to time, the family wears their clothes until they are filthy, and she cooks simple food, mainly beans, steak and potatoes. Once she decides to make cottage cheese out of some milk that has gone bad. It is a

Life on the ranch

lot of work, but when she serves it to the family, they find it so delicious that they gobble it down in a matter of seconds. Lily is appalled that the results of her hard work have disappeared so quickly:

> "'That was the biggest waste of time,' I said. 'I'll never make that mistake again.' Rosemary was eyeing me. 'Let that be a lesson to you,' I told her" (pg. 183).

Rosemary's character

In general, Lily feels there is a lot that her daughter needs to learn: Rosemary is a wild child and quite unlike her mother in character: "I could sense the beginnings of a fundamental difference of opinion between her and me" (ibid.). Although she is still young, Lily wants Rosemary to start learning to read and do math, but Rosemary does not find these things easy. Lily feels the need to make her daughter aware that life can be hard and that she needs to develop a strong character in order to succeed. Jim thinks all of this is too much for a four-year-old, but Lily believes she has to stop Rosemary from being "unfocused" (pg. 184), remembering how many responsibilities she herself had had at that age. She is determined to change Rosemary: "I turned illiterate Mexican kids into readers. I can make my own daughter shape up" (ibid.). However, Rosemary continues to be wild, and seems unable to avoid putting herself in danger. For example, one Halloween her dress catches fire when she gets too close to the candle in the pumpkin. The result is a bad burn on her stomach, but she gets little sympathy from her mother: "Fussing over her wasn't going to help her realize the mistake she'd made" (pg. 185). On the other hand, Rosemary is very brave about her injury, which Lily sees as a positive characteristic.

Rosemary gets badly burnt

During their first winter on the ranch, Jim and Lily invest in a radio that allows them to hear the weather reports. This information from the outside world is absolutely vital to them, letting them know when to expect the huge thunderstorms that will bring the rains to their region. Their children love the rain, which has an almost magical quality in such a dry area, turning the dry earth green. They are allowed to play in the rain and swim in the pool created by Big Jim's Dam, which they

The importance of rain

do for hours on end. Their father teaches them more about the importance of water in all its different forms, how essential to life it is but also how dangerous it can be: "Never take water for granted, Jim said. Always cherish it. Always beware of it" (pg. 188).

The drought

During their second year on the ranch, the rains do not come at all, and by the third year the drought is so serious that all of their water has dried up. Having grown up in the desert, Jim knows that a drought of this kind usually occurs every ten to fifteen years. He has drastically cut back the number of cattle on the ranch, selling off as many as he can and keeping only the healthiest animals. They reach the point when they have to buy water, fetching it in their wagon from a train stop twenty miles away. However, by doing so, they manage to save their remaining cattle, unlike other local ranchers who go bankrupt. The problem is that, when the rain does finally come, it is so heavy and lasts so long that it threatens to wash away the dam. Jim realizes that they need to go out and dig some furrows to drain the water away before it gets to Big Jim. To do so, they have to attach their plow to their pickup truck, which Lily drives while Jim tries to guide the plow in the right direction. Little Jim is placed in a box on the floor of the pickup to keep him safe, and Rosemary stands with her head out of the window of the truck to listen to her father's instructions. The rain is so heavy, though, that she can hardly hear what he is saying, so Lily has to do her best to guess. It is slow, difficult work, but they do what they can – afterwards, all they can do is hope for the best. Their luck is in: the dam holds, while on other ranches cattle are killed and buildings swept away in the flood. The town of Seligman also suffers considerable flood damage. The upside is that, after the rain, the countryside turns green and is covered in beautiful flowers, the likes of which they have never seen before.

The rainstorm following the drought

Saving the dam

VI Teacher Lady

Teacher Lady	
	→ Jim and Lily persuade the Poms to buy the Hackberry ranch, which has its own water supplies. → Wanting to afford a ranch of their own one day, Lily works on various money-making schemes. → She goes back to teaching. → Working in a remote Mormon town, Lily wins the disapproval of the local elders by trying to teach the girls about alternatives to marriage, and loses her job because of it. → In her next teaching job, she also takes on the roles of bus driver and janitor in order to make more money. She loses this job when she physically punishes one of the local deputy's sons.

The need to invest in more land

Luckily for Jim and Lily, the Poms understand that running a ranch is a long-term investment, requiring enough money to survive when things get tough, for example during droughts, and being able to cash in when things improve. The bankruptcies that follow the drought mean that land is available to be bought cheaply. Knowing that what they need is more land with its own water supply, Jim persuades the Poms to buy a neighboring ranch called Hackberry, which includes its own spring and a windmill that pumps water from a well into the cattle troughs. The two ranches together cover 180,000 acres, which means they can raise and sell up to ten thousand cattle a year. They will be able to keep the cattle at Hackberry during the dry winter and drive them to the old ranch in summer, where Big Jim will supply drinking water.

The Poms buy an additional ranch with a good water supply

The Hackberry ranch

The family loves Hackberry right from the start. The land is fertile, and there is a constant supply of water that makes them feel rich. Jim buys some lead pipes and uses them to bring water from the spring to the house, another luxury. Lily paints the house in bring colors, puts rugs on the floors and hangs up curtains. Rosemary also loves colors and is good at drawing what she sees.

Lily and Jim have long dreamt of owning a ranch, and now Lily wants to make that dream a reality by buying

Hackberry. However, she is also determined never to get into debt again, which means they will have to save up the cash they need: she calculates that, with a lot of effort, in ten years they could have enough money. She and Jim had always been careful with money, reusing and recycling wherever possible, but now she begins to find more ideas both for saving money and making some extra cash. She tries selling encyclopedias, taking orders for a mail-order catalog, writing short stories, collecting and selling scrap metal and even playing poker. She and the children drive along Highway 66 at the weekends, picking up old bottles that have been thrown away and collecting the deposit. Not all of her schemes are successful, but gradually her savings grow.

Lily starts saving to buy their own ranch

Another of Lily's unfulfilled ambitions is to learn how to fly. Therefore, when they happen to pass a ranch one day with a small plane and a sign offering flying lessons for $ 5, she gets Jim to stop the car. The pilot of the plane presumes that it is Jim who wants the lesson, and makes the mistake of asking in a rather patronizing tone whether Lily would be able to cope with flying. She quickly puts him in his place, and he agrees to take her up in the plane. Before long they are airborne, Lily enjoying the thrill of flying and waving to her excited family on the ground below. After the lesson, she tells the pilot she will be back for more. Rosemary remarks that they are supposed to be saving money, but Lily replies that there are ways of making money by spending it. She is thinking about getting a pilot's license, which would enable her to earn money by dusting crops and flying rich people from place to place: "'This lesson was an investment,' I said. 'In me'" (pg. 205).

Lily's first flying lesson

Realizing that it will take some time to qualify as a pilot, Lily decides that the best way for her to make some extra cash would be to start working as a teacher again. She therefore inquires about job opportunities, and is offered a position in a remote town on the Arizona Strip called Main Street. Most of the townspeople are Mormons who have moved there so that they can practise polygamy without government interference, but Lily does not mind any of this, and agrees to take the job. She

Lily takes on a new teaching job

takes Rosemary and Little Jim with her, and drives out there, Jim accompanying them to help them move in. Their new home is situated in a tiny town, but the school has a teacherage for her and the children to live in. The townspeople are generally poor, trying to make a living from herding sheep on overgrazed land. Nobody has a car, and the children's clothes have been made from sacks. Once the local people find out that Lily is married to one of Lot Smith's sons, they become very friendly and treat Lily like someone very special.

Mormon girls

The school has thirty students, most of whom are related to each other in some way because their families practise polygamy. The girls have all been entered in the "Joy Book", which means a husband will soon be found for them at the time when their "uncle" thinks they are ready. Lily sees their homes as "breeding factories" (pg. 208) in which up to seven wives are expected to produce a child every year. The young girls are taught to be humble and obedient, and are often married off as young as thirteen. Rosemary is very interested in these other children, their families and their beliefs. Lily tells her that believing something does not make it true. As America is a free country, people can believe whatever they like, and they don't have to believe everything they are told. Rosemary is clever enough to get to the heart of the problem: she asks Lily if the people know that they do not have to believe. This makes Lily think:

> "That, I came to see, was the heart of the matter. You were free to choose enslavement, but the choice was a free one only if you knew what your alternatives were" (pg. 209).

Teaching the girls about alternatives to their Mormon lifestyle

She considers it part of her job to teach the girls in her school about life outside their own little world, about the opportunities that exist and the many things she herself has already done as examples.

The town elder disapproves of her teaching

Unsurprisingly, it is not long before she receives a visit from one of the town's elders, a man known as Uncle Eli. He is an unpleasant man, who keeps patting Lily on the hand and calling her "Teacher Lady" (pg. 210) as he talks to her. He has heard what Lily has been teaching the girls and wants her to stop, explaining that his fellow

Mormons live in this remote place to get away from the wider world. All the girls need is to be able to read the Book of Mormon and do enough math to work out the household budget. Lily responds that her employer is the state of Arizona, not him, and that learning about the wider world must be part of the children's education. Uncle leaves, but not before threatening to put Rosemary's name in the Joy Book, making Lily furious. As a result, the next day Lily gives her students

> "an especially impassioned lesson on political and religious freedom, talking about the totalitarian countries where everyone was forced to believe one thing. In America, by contrast, people were free to think for themselves and follow their hearts when it came to matters of faith" (pg. 212).

Lily teaches the girls that they are free to think for themselves

That evening, she sees Uncle Eli standing outside the teacherage, staring at her. This is repeated the following evening, so Lily makes some curtains out of feed sacks for the window. Later that day, there is a knock at the door. When Lily answers, Uncle Eli is standing outside, staring at her without saying a word. She closes the door, but he begins to knock again. Lily fetches her revolver and opens the door again, pointing her gun at Uncle Eli. Aiming just past his face, she shoots, terrifying him. Lily promises that the next time he knocks at her door like that, she will shoot him. A couple of days later she is visited by the sheriff, who tells her there has been a complaint about her shooting at a resident of the town. Although she explains that she was simply defending herself and her family, the sheriff feels that this is probably not the right place for her if she can't get on with the locals. Lily is therefore not surprised when she receives a letter from the school board ending her contract.

Uncle Eli threatens Lily

Lily loses her job again

Lily is lucky enough to find another teaching job very quickly, in the town of Peach Springs, only sixty-five miles away from the ranch. The teacher's salary is fifty dollars a month, but the county is also looking for a janitor, a bus-driver and a cook, each for ten dollars a month. Lily offers to take on all of these jobs, knowing that she will be able to save a lot of what she earns. Since the county also needs a new school bus, she looks around for possible transport and comes across a second-

Lily gets a new job

She does all the work in the schoolhouse

hand hearse, which she realizes will be perfect for the job. However, although she paints the words "SCHOOL BUS" on the side, everyone still refers to it as 'the hearse'. Lily's new job is hard work. It starts at 4 in the morning with picking up school children, then teaching her students, taking them home again, doing the janitoring duties at the school and finally going home to the ranch. She pays a neighbor five dollars to cook the school lunch. As Rosemary is now seven and Little Jim is five, they come to school with her. Rosemary does not like the fact that her mother is her teacher, partly because Lily spanks her from time to time in front of the class to show them that Rosemary will not receive any special treatment.

Rosemary and Little Jim also attend the school

It takes Lily two journeys to pick up all of the children, leaving the first group at the school while she collects the others. One morning she returns to the school to find Little Jim unconscious, having fallen off a swing. Lily wants to take him to hospital, but the closest one is thirty-five miles away and she does not want to leave the rest of the children on their own while she goes there. So she squeezes as many as she can into and onto the sides of the hearse and takes them back home, planning to drive to the hospital afterwards. After a while, her son regains consciousness and says he feels fine. Angry about the time she has wasted driving around and the possibility of losing a day's pay for canceling the lessons, Lily is determined to go and pick up all the kids again. Rosemary protests that her fellow students will now be enjoying a day off school and won't want to have lessons after all. Lily's response is typical of her: "I've told you before, life's not about doing what you want" (pg. 216). Rosemary's then tries a new tactic, telling her mother that she doesn't feel well and wants to go home. However, Lily decides to take her to hospital instead. Once there, she asks a nurse to put Rosemary in a room on her own overnight, where she will have time to think about what she has done: "If I was going to be docked a day's pay, someone, at the very least, was going to learn a lesson from the experience" (pg. 216). Her plan seems to work, as Rosemary never tries to get out of going to school again.

Little Jim's accident

Lily teaches Rosemary a lesson

Lily's taxi service

Before long, Lily is struck by another money-making opportunity: she can use the hearse as a taxi at weekends. She doesn't have a lot of customers, but there are enough to add to her savings and pay for more flying lessons. She is a good and daring driver; whenever the car gets stuck, all the passengers are expected to get out and push. One group of passengers, three women from Brooklyn who Lily terrifies with her driving, ask Rosemary what Santa Claus is going to bring her, and are perplexed that Rosemary has never heard of him. This makes Lily think. Rancher families seldom celebrated Christmas, not having the time or money for such festivities. However, Lily decides that her family should have a special Christmas this particular year, so she buys some lights and a few toys. On Christmas Day, she gets Jim to climb onto the roof of the ranch while the children are not looking and shake some bells. Lily tells the children it is the sound of St Nicholas who flies around the world with his reindeer, bringing presents to all the children. She hands Rosemary and Little Jim a sock each containing a couple of small gifts. Rosemary does not believe the story of flying reindeer or gifts from the North Pole, so Lily calls Jim back down from the roof. What the children do love, however, are the Christmas lights, which they use to decorate a small tree. The cowboys are also impressed, especially those who have never seen electric lights before. They are a beautiful sight.

Christmas on the ranch

The children do not believe the story of Santa Claus

Six of the students at Lily's school the second year she is working there are Deputy Johnson's children. Although she generally likes the deputy and the way he deals with crime in the town, she knows that he treats anyone who disagrees with him badly. His thirteen children are allowed to do whatever they like and never get into trouble because of their father's position. Johnny Johnson, one of his sons, attends the school and, even at a young age, behaves inappropriately towards girls. Lily dislikes his behavior, thinking he is "a regular tomcat in the making" (pg. 224), but does not do anything about it until he puts his hands up his classmate's skirt. For Lily, he has gone too far and needs to be taught a lesson, so she slaps him in the face. Johnny responds by slapping her in return, convinced that she will not dare to do

Johnny Johnson's sexual behavior

Lily punishes Johnny

anything more to him. He is wrong: Lily gives him a good beating, her anger fuelled by the memory of her first husband and the man who abandoned her sister Helen. She is not surprised, however, when Deputy Johnson comes to see her the next day, to tell her to leave his son alone. She is not intimidated: "[...] I run my classroom, [...] and I'll discipline wayward kids as I see fit" (pg. 226). She knows that the deputy will make sure she is fired and she soon receives a letter telling her that her contract will not be renewed for the coming school year. Lily does not regret what she did, but does not realize how upset she is until Rosemary comes in and finds her crying. Remembering how terrible it had been for her to see her own mother crying, Lily feels she has let her daughter down by putting her in the same position. Therefore she pretends she is not crying at all, but that her eyes are watering because of the dust: "[...] I'm not weak. You'll never have to worry about that. Your mother is not a weak woman" (pg. 227).

Once again, Lily is fired

Importance of not seeming weak

The news that Lily has lost her job soon spreads around the town, with Deputy Johnson telling everyone that he was responsible. She decides to show him and the rest of the townspeople that she is still strong and can hold her head up high. A premiere of *Gone with the Wind* is going to be shown in the nearby town of Kingman, which will be a huge social event, with men in tuxedos and women in long dresses. *Gone with the Wind* is Lily's favorite book: she identifies with Scarlett O'Hara as another tough woman who knows how to get what she wants. Although it is extremely expensive, Lily is determined to go to the premiere, and makes herself a dress out of the red velvet curtains in her living room. She looks "like a movie star" (pg. 229) in the dress, in Rosemary's opinion. Jim drives her to the cinema, although he will not come to see the film with her. So she goes alone and gets her revenge as she steps onto the red carpet and is photographed as if she is indeed a Hollywood star.

Lily at the movie premiere

Lily's revenge

VII The Garden of Eden

The Garden of Eden

- Rosemary and Little Jim are sent away to school, but are unhappy there and do not do well academically.
- Lily goes back to college to finally complete her teaching degree.
- Lily and Rosemary drive to be with Lily's dying father, and bring him back to the KC Ranch to be buried.
- She inherits the land on Salt Draw from her father and decides to keep it as an investment.
- Lily and Rosemary accompany two government inspectors to the village of the Havasupai tribe.
- The valley in which the village is situated is like the Garden of Eden; however, the visit is not a success and Rosemary gets into trouble for shameless behavior.
- The Hackberry ranch is sold to a Hollywood director and Jim loses his job as manager.

Adventures of Rosemary and Little Jim

Rosemary and Little Jim are not allowed to make friends with any of the other schoolchildren in case those friends might expect to be treated differently by Lily. There are no other children living nearby anyway, so the two of them play together most of the time. One of their favorite activities is horse riding, which they have been doing since they were very small. The Poms have sent them a Shetland pony, which is wild and badly behaved, but this does not put Rosemary off: she loves trying to stay on its back. As well as this, she and Little Jim often ride two quarter horses around the ranch, racing the train that runs through their property. Because they are so adventurous, they often hurt themselves, but their parents do not allow them to cry: they have to learn to be tough. One day, Little Jim nearly drowns when he is sucked into a sinkhole in the pond, but his father manages to fish him out and massages his chest until he spits up the muddy water and starts breathing again.

The children are taught to be tough

On another occasion, Lily and Rosemary are out in the pickup when it gets stuck in some mud. They are unable to move it, and there seems to be no alternative to the five-hour walk back to the ranch house, when Lily spots some wild horses and realizes that, if they can catch one, it can pull the truck out for them. There is some horse

Lily and Rosemary catch a wild horse

feed in the pickup, which Lily puts in a bucket, tearing up the sack it was in to make a kind of rope. She and Rosemary approach the horses carefully, Rosemary shaking the bucket with the feed. One of the horses, a mare, shows interest in them, but they know they have to wait for the horse to come to them, and not make eye contact until she does. When the horse is close enough to eat from the bucket, Lily is able to slip the homemade rope over her head and catch her. Rosemary is so thrilled that she was able to get a wild animal to come to her that she wants to keep the horse. Lily sees things differently: "The last thing we need around here is another half-broke horse" (pg. 236), and has Rosemary set the mare free.

Rosemary and Little Jim are sent away to school

When Little Jim is eight and Rosemary is nine, their parents decide that they need some formal schooling and send them away to boarding school. Lily is going to spend the time they are away getting her teaching diploma so that she can get a proper job and join the teacher's union to protect her from being fired all the time. Little Jim is taken to a boys' school in Flagstaff and Rosemary to a Catholic girls' school in Prescott. As she had enjoyed her time at the convent school so much, Lily is sure it will be the same for Rosemary once she gets used to it. She has little sympathy for her daughter's tears: "Some kids would kill for this opportunity! […] Consider yourself lucky!" (pg. 237). She herself goes to Phoenix, registers for some university courses and plans to work for eighteen hours a day to complete her degree. Her life seems much easier than working as a teacher and on the ranch, and she enjoys having nobody else to answer to.

Lily goes back to college

Little Jim and Rosemary do badly at school

Unfortunately, both Little Jim and Rosemary hate school. Little Jim constantly escapes from his school, but does not get into as much trouble as Rosemary, who is seen as a "misfit" (pg. 238). She behaves as wildly as she did at home on the ranch, but at school her behavior seems strange: she is an outsider from the start. She writes to Lily about how much she misses her home and that being at school makes her feel trapped. The nuns do not want to keep her on at school after the first year, but Lily persuades them to give her a second chance. However, when Rosemary's behavior continues to get worse, the Mother Superior refuses to let her come back for a third year. By this time, Lily has completed her degree, and so she collects both children and takes them back to the ranch. They are thrilled to be home.

Rosemary has to leave school

With her qualifications, it is now easy for Lily to get a teaching job, and she registers Rosemary and Little Jim at the school in the town of Big Sandy, where she is now working. Rosemary is very happy not to have to go back to boarding school: "When I grow up, […] all I want to do is live on the ranch and be an artist. That's my dream" (pg. 241). The Second World War has already been going on for some time, but it does not make much difference to the family's lives, apart from the gasoline shortages. By this time, Lily's mother is dead – she died of blood poisoning while Lily was studying in Phoenix, too quickly for her to get home in time to say good-bye. Now Lily gets a telegram from her father, who is in an old people's home and is also dying. He wants Lily to come and get him so that he can be with his family again. It is a long journey, and the problem is that, since fuel is rationed, she will not be able to buy enough gasoline to get her there and back. She is sure, however, that she will find a way to make sure her father does not have to die alone. She swaps meat for some additional gasoline coupons and sets off with Rosemary, also taking a gas can and some hose.

Lily gets a new teaching job at Big Sandy

Lily's father is dying

On the journey, Lily and Rosemary do their best to keep cheerful. When they reach the town of Tempe, they are almost out of gas and have no more coupons to buy more. Lily parks at a truck stop and goes into the diner, which is full of men in cowboy hats. Lily makes an announcement, telling the men about the reason for her journey and asking if some of them will give her some gas so that she can continue on her way. Many of them do so, and before long the tank is two-thirds full again. Lily is very proud of her resourcefulness. The next day they reach Tucson and go to the old people's home where Dad is living. He looks very ill, and tells Lily he won't make it home now:

The journey to collect her father and take him home to the KC Ranch

> "'Looks like I'm going to die here [...] but I don't want to be buried here. Promise me you'll take my body back to the KC.'
> 'I promise.'
> Dad smiled. 'I could always count on you'" (pg. 244)

Dad dies the same night that Lily gets there

He dies the same night, as if all he had been waiting for was for Lily to come and promise to take him back to the ranch.

The next day, Dad's body is carried out to the car and they set off on their journey back to the KC Ranch. This time, it is more urgent that they travel quickly, before Dad's body starts to decompose. Once again, they have to stop to ask for gas, but when Lily explains she's traveling with her father's body, which needs to be buried as soon as possible, the startled men are keen to give her what she needs. Back at the KC Ranch, Dad is buried in the small cemetery there in his special hat. Lily is not upset about his death like she was about Helen's: nobody had expected him to survive his childhood accident, but he had, and had managed to live a good life: "He hadn't drawn the best of cards, but he'd played his hand darned well, so what was there to grieve over?" (pg. 246).

Dad is buried at home

Lily's inheritance

Buster has inherited the KC Ranch and Lily the homestead on Salt Draw, on which several thousand dollars' worth of tax are still owed. Lily has to decide whether to sell this land and use the money to pay the taxes, or to pay the taxes with the money they've saved to buy the Hackberry ranch. Back home, she talks it through with Jim, but by now she has become convinced that they should not sell. Land is a good investment, and oil is now being found in Texas, so its value might rise considerably if oil is discovered on their property. But it is more than this: the land has been in her family for generations and she shares her father's and grandfather's desire to own something solid, something to call her own:

> "And if the world went to hell in a handbasket – as it seemed to be doing – you could say good-bye to everyone and retreat to your land, hunkering down and living off it. Land belonged to you and yours forever" (pg. 248).

Jim is still skeptical, as the land is not good for cattle and they would not be able to have a large herd. It would also use up a large part of their savings. However, Lily points out that they might never be able to afford Hackberry, but the land on Salt Draw is theirs for sure. So they pay off what is owed and become "bona fide Texas land barons" (ibid.).

They decide to keep the land on Salt Draw

Because of the war, the cattle roundup has been delayed for a few months, as the railways are needed to transport soldiers. Since a lot of their cowboys have gone off to fight, Rosemary, Little Jim and Lily lend a hand. Although the children have been going to roundups all their lives, they are not allowed to do the roughest jobs, but are outriders, rounding up the cattle who have escaped from the main herd. Although Rosemary enjoys roundups, she does not like the idea of the cattle being killed, and is happy when one of them manages to get away, secretly hoping it won't be recaptured. One day, when she is sent to round up a stray steer, she comes back to say she cannot find it. Jim sends one of the cowboys, a Havasupai boy called Fidel Hanna, to look for the steer, and shortly afterwards he returns with the animal. Jim is annoyed with Rosemary, who pretends innocence throughout the incident, and Fidel defends her, saying that the steer was hiding. Only Lily notices the wink he gives Rosemary, and from that day onwards she can see that her daughter has a crush on Fidel. He is young and good-looking, and Rosemary, now aged thirteen, is also becoming very attractive. Lily realizes she will have to be careful from now on and make sure nothing happens between the two young people.

The cattle roundup

Rosemary and Fidel

While the cattle are being loaded onto the railway cars, two young ones escape, much to Rosemary's delight. After they are recaptured, Lily has a sharp word with her daughter: if she wants to live on the ranch when she is older, as she says she does, she has to accept that what ranchers do is raise cattle to be killed for food: "If that upsets you – if you're rooting for the cattle to break free – you're not cut out for ranch life" (pg. 252). Back on the ranch, to Lily's surprise, Rosemary announces that she wants to learn how do to the very unpleasant job of skin-

Rosemary wants the cattle to be free

She learns to skin a steer

ning a young cow after it has been slaughtered. She says that she needs to know how to do it as she is going to be a rancher. Therefore, the next time a steer is killed, Rosemary helps to cut it up for meat. She does her best to be brave about it, but cannot help crying as she cuts the skin from the dead animal's body. She keeps working until the task is finished, but then washes her hands and walks away from the meat house without speaking. At that moment, Jim and Lily realize something about their daughter:

> "We both knew that she'd proved she could do it, but she'd also proved that she didn't truly have the heart for it, and none of us ever mentioned it again" (pg. 253).

A visit from the Education Department

The next summer, a superintendent working for the Arizona Department of Education called Clarice Pearl announces that she will be coming to the area with a nurse to check up on the living conditions of the Havasupai children who live in a village near the ranch. Lily is to drive them to the canyon and organize horses and a guide for the rest of the journey to the village. As it happens, Fidel Hanna comes from that village and lives there part of the time, so Lily asks him to organize the trip. He laughs when he hears about the intentions of these two white women, knowing that their visit will not do any good. The arrangements are made, and Lily goes with Rosemary to collect Miss Pearl and Marion Finch, the nurse, to take them to the village. She senses immediately how things are going to go when she sees the women:

> "I recognized the type – disapproving do-gooders. They always had very high standards, and they always let you know that you didn't quite measure up to them" (pgs. 254–255).

They drive to where they have agreed to meet Fidel, but there is nobody around. Suddenly, a group of young Indians, dressed in traditional costume, "whooping and brandishing spears" (pg. 255) appear on horseback and circle the women threateningly. However, Lily recognizes that the leader is Fidel, and shouts at him to stop. He and

Fidel plays a trick

the other young men think the joke they have played is hilarious, but Miss Pearl and Miss Finch are not amused. Three of the horses are for the three adult women; Fidel tells Rosemary she can go with him, pulling her up onto his horse and riding off before Lily can protest.

They arrive at the village

It takes Miss Pearl, Miss Finch and Lily a long time to reach the village, with their horses moving at walking pace rather than galloping, as the path is steep and winding. The scenery is beautiful: green and lush with lots of streams and springs that turned into waterfalls further on. There are pools of clear, turquoise water at the Havasupai village, where several children are swimming, naked. Fidel and his friends dive in, too, and Rosemary wants to join them; however, her mother will not let her swim in her underwear, and she does not have a bathing suit with her. There is a guest hut where the four of them can stay; Miss Pearl and Miss Finch want to rest, but Lily and Rosemary take up Fidel's offer of a tour of the valley. The place where the Havasupai live is beautiful but remote. The white settlers forced them to change their hunting habits, so they now live here, hidden away: "a secret, hidden tribe living life the ancient way while most people on the outside world didn't even know it existed" (pg. 258). There are two pillars of rock high above the cliff wall, which the tribe calls the Wigleeva. They believe that the Wigleeva protect them and that anyone who leaves permanently will be turned to stone. Rosemary is captivated, and feels that she would like to live there forever, although only people who have been born into the Havasupai tribe are allowed to do so. Fidel suggests that she might become the first white woman to marry into the tribe.

Rosemary wants to swim with the Havasupai children

The beautiful valley

Trying to impose an Anglo lifestyle on the children does no good

In the evening, the two women from the education department refuse to eat the traditional food offered to them by the tribespeople. The next day Miss Finch checks the health of the children, and Miss Pearl talks to their parents about suitable education for them. Although the village has a schoolhouse, it is considered inadequate, and sometimes representatives of the state visit and take children away to boarding school, where they are supposed to receive an education that will make them fit better into the white world. Fidel tells Rosemary that it is no good taking the children away, as it turns them into misfits who are neither at home in the valley or in the outside world. He is speaking from personal experience, as he is one of the children who were forced to go to that school. He feels that, because of this, he has turned to stone on the inside. Rosemary, however, is still in love with the place and imagines herself living there, calling it "the Garden of Eden" (pg. 259). Lily is more pragmatic, and warns her daughter: "Don't idealize this way of life [...] I was born in a dirt house, and you get tired of it pretty quickly" (ibid.). That night, Lily is woken by a lot of noise and gets up to discover Rosemary, soaking wet and wrapped in a blanket, outside the hut being shouted at by Miss Pearl. Apparently Miss Pearl had woken up, gone outside for some fresh air and found Rosemary swimming in the pool with Fidel and some of the other Havasupai kids. Rosemary protests that she was wearing her underwear, but this does not make any difference as far as Miss Pearl is concerned. Lily is so angry that Rosemary has disobeyed her in this way, and possibly put herself into danger, that she completely loses control. She takes her belt and whips her daughter "until I had the sickening feeling that I'd gone too far" (pg. 260).

Rosemary sees the valley as the "Garden of Eden"

Rosemary goes swimming at night with some of the Havasupai

Lily punishes Rosemary for her wild behavior

The next day, the four white women make the return journey, Lily and Rosemary not speaking. That evening, Lily tries to speak to her daughter about what happened, saying that the beating was necessary in order to teach her a lesson. Rosemary responds, "All I learned is that when I have children, I'm never going to whip them" (pg. 261). All in all, no good has come of their trip to the "Garden of Eden". Fidel, afraid that Miss Pearl will carry out her threat to have him arrested, joins the army, but the war gives him shell shock, and he goes on a shooting spree shortly after leaving the army. Luckily, he does not kill anyone, but is sent to prison and, after his release, is shunned by his village because of what he has done. He ends up living alone in a remote place: "He had, in the end, turned to stone" (ibid.). The other consequence of the trip is that Lily feels she can no longer trust her fourteen-year-old daughter on the ranch where there are several young men, and therefore decides that Rosemary has to go back to boarding school. She does not want to: once again, she suffers greatly from homesick-

Fidel becomes an outcast

Rosemary is sent away to school again

ness, gets bad grades and seems to be just a dreamer who spends most of her time drawing. However, Lily feels this is the best place for her for now.

The ranch is to be sold

They cannot afford to buy the ranch

Just after all of this happens, another, much bigger problem arises for Jim and Lily. The Poms write to them to tell them that the ranch is going to be sold so that they can invest in the munitions industry instead. They are prepared to give Jim first option to buy, if they can find more investors, but they are going to sell the ranch no matter what happens. Although Jim and Lily have managed to save quite a lot of money, it is not enough, and they cannot find anyone prepared to enter into a partnership with them – the war is taking its toll on everyone by now. There are very few people with money to spend, but now Lily and Jim get to meet one of them. A car with three men in it arrives at the ranch one day: one is wearing a suit, one a safari jacket and leather gaiters and the third has on a big cowboy hat, jeans and snakeskin boots.

The new owner arrives

> "Suit introduced himself as the Poms' lawyer. Gaiters turned out to be a movie director famous for his westerns who was interested in buying the ranch. Boots was some rodeo cowboy Gaiters had cast in a few bit parts" (pg. 263).

Lily does not take to Gaiters, as she calls him, as he is "one of those people who acted as if everything that came out of his mouth, even the most obvious remark, was profoundly interesting" (ibid.). Suit and Boots agree with everything he says. They pay no attention to Jim, who is showing them around, but instead talk about what they are going to change and add to the place, such as an airstrip so that they can fly in from Hollywood. They also want to get more cattle and even breed horses. It is clear that they have absolutely no idea how to run a ranch, but have an idealized view of what one should be like. According to Gaiters, Jim does not look like a cowboy and the ranch does not look like a ranch: it is lacking "magic" (pg. 264). Before long, Gaiters has changed the ranch to match his idea of what one should look like. He has the buildings pulled down and rebuilt, and fires Jim, Old Jake and all the Mexican and Indian cowboys because none of them look the part. Lily and Jim are upset

The new owner makes a lot of changes

by the changes: although the ranch has never belonged to them, they have always done a good job of running it and taken good care of it. Jim is particularly unhappy, as he has been given the feeling that he is no longer needed, but Lily does not let him get depressed: "We've never felt sorry for ourselves before [...] and we're not going to start now. Let's get packing" (pg. 266).

Jim loses his job

The family have saved up enough money to make a new start, and decide to move to a city this time. They choose Phoenix as an up-and-coming place with plenty of new opportunities. Both of the children are upset about leaving, but Lily tells them they have no choice in the matter. They sell off nearly everything they own connected to ranching, and Lily gives Patches, her old horse, to the Havasupai so that she can end her days in the Garden of Eden. Everything else fits into the back of the hearse, and as they drive away, Lily tells Little Jim not to look back.

The family moves to Phoenix

VIII Gumshoes

Gumshoes	
	➟ The family moves to Phoenix to try city life, but finds it difficult to adapt. ➟ Rosemary wants to become an artist; Lily is skeptical about this as a career choice. ➟ Jim does not enjoy his new desk job and is delighted when he is asked to help out on various ranches during a severe spell of winter. ➟ Lily thinks Jim might be having an affair. However, when she and Rosemary "investigate", it turns out not to be true. The family decides that they need to leave the city.

Some new purchases

Just after their move to Phoenix, Jim suggests they treat themselves to something special. Lily immediately knows what she wants: a set of dentures. As going to the dentist has a low priority in the remote areas in which they have been living, both her and Jim's teeth are in a terrible state, so they visit a dentist who pulls all of their remaining teeth and replaces them with a set of new dentures. Lily is delighted at the result, and often pulls out her false teeth to show other people. In addition to the teeth, they buy a large house and a new car, getting rid of the old hearse.

City life is very different to life on the ranch

Lily loves living in Phoenix at first and makes the most of living in a big city. However, the rest of her family sees it differently, feeling trapped in the city and missing life on the ranch. After a few months, Lily begins to agree with them. Living in a city makes her feel "penned in" (pg. 274). She can no longer do more or less what she wants, for example when driving, as all the traffic rules limit her freedom to drive how she likes. She misses flying, but when she tries to book more lessons, here too she is confronted with regulations that have to be met before she can take to the air again. One advantage of the city, however, is that there are plenty of jobs, so neither she nor Jim have any trouble finding work. They also find plenty of investment opportunities, buying houses to rent out. On the whole, though, Lily finds there is much more to worry about, living in a city, especially crime, which makes her nervous. "On the ranch, we worried about the weather and the cattle and horses, but we never worried about ourselves" (pg. 276).

Life is full of worries

The atom bomb

At this time, bombs are another reason for people to worry. The atom bomb has just been dropped on Hiroshima, and Rosemary gets very upset at the thought of all the innocent people and animals that have been killed. Lily's viewpoint is that the Japanese were the ones who started the war and now no more American soldiers will have to die. The images of Hiroshima and Nagasaki give Rosemary nightmares, and she becomes very afraid of the power that the atom bomb gives to those who are able to use it.

Rosemary wants to become an artist

Lily begins to worry about what Rosemary will do for a living, as all she seems to be good at, and interested in, is painting and drawing. She shows no talent for playing a musical instrument or modeling, despite her good looks, so eventually Lily gives in to her wish to become an artist and signs her up for lessons with a teacher called Ernestine. Rosemary enjoys the lessons and becomes even more enthusiastic about the power of art. She starts to write her name as Rose Mary as she thinks

Lily does not enjoy teaching in the city

it looks nicer. Although Lily carries on paying for the lessons, she always emphasizes to her daughter that being a nurse, a secretary or a teacher are still the only real career options for women, the best being teaching. Ironically, at this time Lily does not really like her job. Having been used to more or less being her own boss, she finds it difficult to work in a large school where many of the pupils come from wealthy families and do not show her any respect. When one of the other teachers notices that she is carrying a pistol in her handbag, she is horrified, and reports Lily to the principal. He says he will fire her if she brings the gun to school again; Lily cannot understand what the fuss is about.

Jim misses his old life

Like Lily, Jim is unhappy in his new job. He now has a rather boring desk job in a warehouse where he does not have to work very hard, certainly not in comparison to on the ranch, and as a result often spends time chatting with the bookkeeper, who Lily describes as "a tarted-up divorcée I did not take to named Glenda" (pg. 282). He misses his old outdoor lifestyle, and is still skilful at interpreting the natural world. For example, he can see that the coming winter is going to be severe. It seems strange to him and Lily that, living in the city, the bad weather does not make any additional work for them. On the ranch, they would have had to protect the animals from the snow and make sure none of them died of cold, whereas in the city they only have to turn up the heating. As it turns out, many ranchers are not prepared for the snow, and before long Jim gets a visit from the Arizona Department of Agriculture, desperately looking for him as they need him to help them out. He does not need to be asked twice:

> "Jim threw some heavy clothes into his old army duffel bag, grabbed his hat, and was out the door in less than five minutes" (pg. 284).

He helps to save several herds

Back on the range, Jim arranges for hay to be dropped off by plane to the ranches that need it. He flies to the most remote ranches and gives the ranchers instructions on how to save their herds, for example by breaking the ice on ponds so that the cattle can still drink, and keeping them moving so that their blood can circulate. At one ranch, it is not possible for the plane to land, so Jim parachutes out it, although he has never done used a parachute before. He also visits his old workplace, now called the Showtime Ranch, and finds it in a sorry state. Thousands of cattle have died of cold, and the new ranch hands are not doing anything about it, but instead are sitting around drinking coffee. He makes them break the ice and get the remaining cattle moving and fed. All in all, Jim is away from home for two weeks, and when he comes back he has lost weight, his hands are sore and he is exhausted:

Jim is happy again

> "But he was happy. He hadn't felt this useful since leaving the ranch. He'd been out doing what he was meant to do. He was Big Jim again" (pg. 285).

He is offered his old job back

One consequence of Jim's actions is that Gaiters calls him, offering him his old job back. However, while Jim was back around the region of the ranch, he'd heard that Gaiters had always called him a "relic" (pg. 286), and it is only since the snowstorm that he has changed his tune. Jim and Lily decide not to go back to the ranch, as they would still have to do whatever Gaiters told them rather than run it themselves. They want to keep their independence.

Jim and Glenda

Jim is now something of a local hero and is known as the "Parachutin' Cowboy" (pg. 287). He is slightly embarrassed by the attention; Lily notices that a lot of this attention comes from women, who now often behave flirtatiously toward him. One day, she goes to see him at the warehouse and finds him talking to Glenda, who, to Lily's fury, is not embarrassed to see her, but continues to flirt with Jim. He is obviously uncomfortable, and Lily is determined to "keep an eye on the two of them" (ibid.).

Lily's mistrust of Jim

Lily's experience with her first husband has made her mistrustful of men, even of someone like Jim, and she cannot stop asking herself whether Jim might really be having an affair with Glenda. The more she thinks about it, the more she feels the need to know the truth, one way or another. Not wanting to hire a gumshoe, and reluctant to spy on her husband herself, she decides to get Rosemary to help her. Rosemary is not keen on the idea,

Rosemary and Lily as gumshoes

but Lily persuades her by saying that she is not going to be spying on her father, but simply carrying out an investigation to hopefully prove his innocence. Lily thinks that, if something is going on between Jim and Glenda, they will probably be meeting at lunchtimes. Therefore, on the first day, she parks the car near the warehouse and sends Rosemary to follow Jim when he goes on his lunch break, making a note of everything he does. When Rosemary returns, half an hour later, she can only report that her father bought himself some lunch from a grocery store and then sat in the park to eat it. On the second day, Lily has not been waiting long when Rosemary returns with Jim. He wants an explanation, so Lily confesses her worries that he might be cheating on her.

Jim is innocent

Jim does not say much at the time, but that evening he sits down for a talk with Lily. He is not cheating on her, and explains that she must trust him, as, living in a city, it is not possible to avoid other women all the time. They both come to the conclusion that city life may be getting too much for them, and that they need to move on.

IX The Flyboy

→ The family move to Horse Mesa, a tiny, remote village, where they feel happy again. → Rosemary meets Rex, a wild young air force pilot, who tells her on their first meeting that they are going to get married. → Rosemary is fascinated by Rex because he is wild and unpredictable. → Lily disapproves of Rex – she sees him as unreliable and not the right person for her daughter. → Rex takes Lily flying – although she comes to understand him better, she still thinks he is unsuitable for her daughter. → Despite her mother, Rosemary marries Rex: the two of them have an unconventional lifestyle.	The Flyboy

The family moves from Phoenix to a small, extremely remote place called Horse Mesa. It is so small that there are only thirteen families living there, but they have a school and Lily gets the job of teacher. The road leading to Horse Mesa is narrow, winding and dangerous, but Lily loves it, seeing it as her escape route from "the traffic jams, news bulletins, bureaucrats, air-raid sirens, and locked doors of city life" (pg. 296). The scenery is dramatic, and the few houses of Horse Mesa are located next to a blue lake. The place is so remote that groceries have to be transported there by truck twice a week, and any phone calls have to be booked in advance and made in the community center. However, the family loves the town right from the start. Jim gets a job repairing roads, working outdoors once more, and Lily is happy to be back working as an independent teacher.

Escape from city life

The family is happy again

As the school in Horse Mesa only takes children up to the eighth grade, once again Rosemary and Little Jim have to be sent away to school. Lily and Jim enjoy the slow pace and simple lifestyle of the small town, where all the inhabitants have to get along with each other. However, Lily's strong personality does not allow her to sit quietly at home: she becomes involved in politics, helping to prevent the closure of some local schools and

Lily gets involved in politics

making sure that all of the residents of Horse Mesa are registered to vote, and then that they do so when elections are held.

Little Jim gets married

Rosemary and Little Jim have now both finished school and go on to Arizona State University. By now, Little Jim is bigger than his father. He enjoys playing football at college but is not really interested in studying. He is still in his first year there when he meets and marries a girl called Diane, leaving college to become a police officer. Rosemary is still a cause for concern for her mother, mainly because of their different attitudes to life. She has been allowed to study art at the university, but only if she also qualifies as a teacher. A lot of men ask her out on dates, and even propose to her, but Lily wants her to wait for the right man. In her opinion, the right man for her daughter would be someone who would have a steadying influence on her:

Lily's opinion on the right husband for her daughter

> "That girl still had a tendency to be flighty, but with a solid man beside her, I could see her settling down, teaching elementary school, raising a couple of kids, and dabbling in painting on the side" (pg. 301).

Lily is sure that she will find a man for Rosemary; however, things do not work out that way. One summer she meets a young pilot from the air force while swimming in a canyon with some friends. He jumps into the water after her, although he cannot swim very well, and tells her that they are going to get married, not as a proposal, but as a statement of fact. His name is Rex Walls, and Rosemary is fascinated by him right from the start. He is daring, somewhat aggressive, very talkative and, something that particularly appeals to Rosemary, he is interested in seeing her artwork.

Rosemary meets Rex, a 'flyboy'

Shortly after they first meet, Rex comes to Horse Mesa to see Rosemary's paintings. He seems to genuinely admire them, and insists on taking down the two paintings Lily has on the living room wall and replacing them with two of Rosemary's originals. Rosemary loves the praise he gives her, but Lily does not really trust him: "He was charming, but most con men were, since before they fleeced you, they needed to gain your trust"

Lily and Jim meet Rex

(pg. 305). Before long, Rosemary and Rex are a couple. Like his wife, Jim thinks that Rex is "all talk" (pg. 305). Lily knows that if she forbids Rosemary to see Rex, he will only seem more attractive to her, but she tries to warn her daughter about the kind of man Rex is: "'He's not exactly a rock,' I said. 'I don't want to marry a rock,' she said" (ibid.). Instead, one of the things Rosemary likes about him is that anything can happen while they are together, that nothing about him is predictable.

Lily does not want Rosemary to get serious about Rex

One day, Rex turns up at the house and announces that he wants to learn to ride a horse, as they are all so skilled at horsemanship. So Lily, Jim and Rosemary take him to a local family that has some horses they can ride. It has been a while since the horses were last ridden, and it is difficult even to catch them. Rosemary chooses one of the wildest ones, and Rex also insists on an animal with spirit, wanting to gallop off before he has even learnt to ride properly. He frightens the horse, which has to be calmed down by Lily before it will stop; inevitably, Rex gets thrown, but is able to laugh it off and get back on for another try. That evening, after they have eaten, Lily suggests playing poker. Rex agrees eagerly, and contributes a bottle of whiskey to the party. After her long years of experience, Lily is able to judge a man's character accurately by the way he plays poker. She discovers that Rex is a good poker player, but, as the evening progresses, he drinks more and more whiskey, losing his good judgment in the process and becoming very angry when Lily wins. He is rather rude to her, which appeals to Rosemary: "he was the first fellow she'd brought home who hadn't been even a little bit scared of me" (pg. 311). When he gets up to leave, they try to prevent him from going, as he is very drunk and the road is dangerous. However, he refuses: "Rex Walls don't take orders from anyone" (pg 312) and drives away.

Rex learns to ride

Rex plays poker with the family

He drives home while drunk

Lily now feels it is time to talk to Rosemary about Rex in no uncertain terms, but she does not make any impression on her daughter. Rosemary is well aware of what Rex is like, but feels that the world is dangerous anyway, and what she wants from life is adventure, not security.

Rosemary does not want a life of security

Lily comes to realize that Rosemary has never really listened to her, and feels that she has failed in the way she has brought her daughter up. The same day, Rex returns to the house, with a bunch of lilies that he gives to Lily to show he is sorry for his behavior. He also has another kind of peace-offering for her: he says he will take her up in his plane. This is an offer Lily finds impossible to resist. On the way to the plane, he tells her more about his background, and they find that they have some things in common: for example, he also helped to sell illegal alcohol when he was young. Rex is not actually allowed to take Lily, a civilian, up in a military plane, but this is a rule that many pilots ignore. He has to go and get a plane from the airbase and then pick Lily up from a field behind a friend's trailer so that no-one at the base will see what he is doing. Once up in the air, she remembers everything she loves about flying. Rex even lets her take over the controls for a while, then takes over again and proceeds to do a number of aerial tricks: flying very low over tree tops and under telephone wires, making Lily even more convinced that he is crazy. His only response is to laugh: "That's what your daughter loves about me!" (pg. 318).

Rex takes Lily flying

Before much longer, Rosemary and Rex announce that they are going to get married. Lily still thinks she is making the wrong choice, but Rosemary is determined to marry him, no matter what her mother thinks. Rex is going to leave the air force, and instead he and Rosemary are going to carry out some of his "big plans" (pg. 319). Jim accepts his daughter's decision, and tries to make Lily see that Rosemary is doing what is best for her, even though things have not turned out the way Lily would have liked:

Rex and Rosemary get engaged

> "People are just like animals […] Some are happiest penned in, some need to roam free. You got to recognize what's in her nature and accept it" (pg. 320).

He points out that Rosemary is actually quite lucky: she knows what she wants to do, i.e. to paint, and she has found love. Because of this, she is better off than many people. If Lily can accept this, she will feel better.

Lily says she will pay for the wedding if the young couple gets married in a Catholic Church. She wants them to have a traditional wedding, in the hope that it might encourage them to live a more traditional lifestyle than the one they seem to be planning. They book a hotel, buy Rosemary a beautiful wedding dress and invite all their friends and acquaintances. The newlyweds do not make any honeymoon plans, but are instead just going to drive off "and go where the road takes us" (pg. 321).

Lily plans the wedding

It is a beautiful wedding, with lots of drinking and dancing, and everyone has a good time. Afterwards, the whole wedding party goes out onto the street to see the couple off. They drive away "like a couple of half-broke horses" (pg. 322).

The wedding

EPILOGUE The Little Critter

The Little Critter

- The family after Rosemary's wedding
- Rosemary and Rex live an unsettled life and start having children
- Jeannette Walls is born – Lily is determined to play an important part in her granddaughter's life

Lily and Jim stay on in Horse Mesa. Although Jim has retired from his job, he finds plenty to do as the "unofficial mayor" (pg. 325), and is always happy to lend his neighbors a hand. Lily carries on teaching, unable to imagine a life where she would have nothing to do all day.

Jim retires; Lily keeps working

Little Jim and his wife Diane are now living a stable life in a suburb of Phoenix, and have a couple of children. Rosemary and Rex, on the other hand, have anything but a conventional lifestyle. They move around the desert instead of making a permanent home somewhere. Rex is still pursuing his "various harebrained schemes" (ibid.), earning a bit of money to live off in the meantime by doing odd jobs. Rosemary works hard at her painting and soon has children, too. The first two are girls, although one of them dies of cot death before her first birthday. Their third child, another girl, is born in

Rosemary's married life

Phoenix, and since they don't have any money to pay their hospital bill, Lily has to pay it for them, giving her another reason to get annoyed with Rex.

Jeannette is born

The new baby is called Jeannette. She is not a particularly pretty child, but has "smiling green eyes and the beginnings of a strong, square jaw just like mine" (pg. 326). Lily feels a connection to her granddaughter from the start. She knows that Rosemary and Rex's children are going to have a lot of unusual experiences because of their parents, but she is sure that, with their family background, they will be tough enough to deal with whatever life brings them. And, in addition to this, she will always be around to teach her grandchildren what she thinks they need to know.

The Characters

Lily Casey Smith

	Lily Casey Smith
➞ The feisty protagonist of the story leads an extremely varied life with lots of adventures. ➞ She qualifies as a teacher, manages ranches and marries twice. ➞ She goes through life with a determination to make the best of things and to win through against the odds – generally, she succeeds.	

In the words of Jeannette Walls, her granddaughter and biographer, Lily Casey Smith is "quite a character" (pg. 327). It is hard to disagree with this statement. Throughout her life, Lily experiences hardship, adventure, disappointment and success, and has the determination and resourcefulness to get through every situation she is faced with. The story is narrated in the first person, so we the readers see everything from her point of view. This gives us insight into her character, both through her actions and the opinions she expresses. On the whole, she comes across as a likable person, certainly as one who deserves our admiration for making her way in life, often against the odds. The constant need to overcome problems makes her very tough, but also very self-confident. This means that she is not someone who suffers fools gladly, or is particularly tolerant of people with different opinions to her own. Her relationship with her daughter Rosemary illustrates this particularly clearly. One thing that Jeannette Walls does not do is romanticize her grandmother's life or character. She allows Lily to describe things as they really were, speaking in her own "distinctive voice" (pg. 328), and thereby creating a very vivid picture of her life for the reader.

First-person narrative

An admirable character

Lily speaks in her own voice

Even as a child, when it comes to coping with problems Lily shows the kind of resourcefulness that makes her seem mature beyond her years. In the very opening scene of the book, the reader discovers her bravery and

She is brave and quick-thinking

ability to think quickly, when she saves herself, her brother and her sister from a flash flood. Not only does she immediately realize that there will not be enough time to get back home and they will have to take refuge in a tree, but she manages to stop her siblings from falling asleep, and thereby falling out of the tree and being swept away by the flood water. Her determination to survive gets them through the night; however, she knows that only they can bring about their own survival – there will be no outside help: "It would happen – but it was up to us to make it happen" (pg. 15). She has this attitude throughout her life: if she wants something done, it will be up to her to see that it happens.

Responsible for her own survival

Money-making schemes

This resourcefulness in finding solutions continues to serve her well throughout her life. For example, Lily is good at coming up with money-making schemes, either to help solve financial difficulties or to save up for the future. Selling bootleg liquor keeps her and Jim's garage afloat until it becomes too dangerous to continue. When trying to save up to buy a ranch of their own, she never misses an opportunity to make or save money: making chairs out of orange crates, reusing everything they can, even collecting bottles that have been thrown away in order to get the deposit back. She does this so eagerly that Jim, her husband, is a little embarrassed when their daughter starts fishing old bottles out of someone else's trash, but Lily is proud of her: every cent they save adds up and, as she says, "I'm teaching them resourcefulness" (pg. 202). Perhaps one of the most moving examples is when she needs to travel a long distance to reach her dying father. Due to fuel rationing, it will be difficult to get enough gasoline for the journey there and back, but Lily is determined to find a way: she will "[b]eg, borrow, or steal" (pg. 242) what she needs. As it turns out, she is able to persuade some truckers to top up her gas tank so that she can complete her journey. She finds the right words to appeal to their good nature, and so manages to see her father before he dies, take him back to his ranch to be buried, and make the journey home, all without having enough fuel coupons.

Ways of saving money

She teaches her children to be resourceful

She is persuasive when it comes to getting what she needs

Lily is fiercely independent. From a young age, she has always had to think for herself and get things done without much outside help. For example, while still living with her parents on the ranch, she is often the one who has to run the place, doing a lot of the physical work because her father is limited by his physical disabilities and her mother "wasn't exactly the most useful person in the world" (pg. 34) when it came to being practical. She sees it as her job "to keep the place from falling apart" (pg. 35). This independent self-sufficiency stays with her for the rest of her life. One striking example of this is when, aged just fifteen, she rides from the ranch to Red Lake, a journey that takes a month, to start her job at the school there. She travels alone, sleeping in the open, with just a small gun given to her by her father for protection. Later, she travels to Chicago, again alone, and has to make her way there. In some ways, Lily could be said to be an early feminist. Born at a time when young women were expected to get married and stay at home rather than have a career, which is what her parents expect of her and her sister, she cannot imagine taking that path: "No man had proposed to me yet, and if I sat around waiting for one, I could well end up as that potato-peeling spinster in the corner of the kitchen" (pg. 91). Lily, however, is determined to do something useful with her life.

Used to hard physical work from a young age

Unafraid to travel alone, even as a young woman

Lily is a feminist

She wants to do something practical rather than wait to get married

Even when she does get married, she manages to maintain her independence, especially during her second marriage to Jim Smith. She insists that their married life must be an equal partnership and not a relationship in which she has to rely on him for everything. Jim respects this by never telling her what to do or expecting her to stay obediently at home. Indeed, some of the time she takes on teaching jobs where she has to work and live away from the ranch, taking care of herself and her children without the permanent protection of a man in the house.

Still independent even as a married woman

Throughout her life, Lily shows a love of learning. As a young child on Salt Draw and at the KC Ranch, she is taught at home by her father. They cover all kinds of subjects: "grammar, history, arithmetic, science, and

Her love of learning

civics" (pg. 31). She is fascinated by science and geometry because she "loved learning that there were these invisible rules that explained the mysteries of the world we lived in" (ibid.). We often see examples of her eagerness to learn, and to make the most of opportunities to educate herself further. At her convent school in Santa Fe, she reads "every book I could get my hands on" (pg. 55), and, while at college in Flagstaff, she wishes she "could take every course in the curriculum and read every book in the library" (pg. 116). Because she has to work so hard to get an education at all, and to earn the money to pay for it, she appreciates the opportunities she is given to learn, and makes the most of them. She is generally older than the other students, but works much harder than them and is very focused on her studies. Being at college means freedom for her, freedom to do something that she wants to do rather than working for the benefit of others: "I had no obligations to anyone but myself, and everything in my life was under my control" (pg. 237).

Making the most of opportunities for education

Being at college means doing something for herself rather than for others

In addition to this, Lily is a teacher herself for a large part of her life. As a child on her parents' ranch, she passes on what she has learnt from her father to her brother and sister, and later tutors weaker students at the boarding school she attends. However, she does not consider joining the teaching profession until the principal of her school, Mother Albertina, suggests it to her, and she realizes that it would be ideal for her: "I loved books. I loved learning. I loved that 'Eureka!' moment when someone finally figured something out" (pg. 57). Therefore, when Mother Albertina writes to tell her about the test she can take in order to become a teacher, she jumps at the chance. In the years that follow, Lily does not work continually as a teacher, but it is something that she always comes back to. Her teaching style is strict: she expects obedience and respect, but is also convinced that it is possible to teach all children, even the weaker ones: "Every kid [is] good at something, and the trick was to find out what it was, then use it to teach him everything else" (pg. 85). The way she teaches has clearly been colored by her experience in breaking horses. Here obedience is vital if the horse is to learn to

Even as a child she teaches her siblings

She returns to teaching at different points in her life

Teaching is compared to horse-breaking

take a saddle and become a useful working animal. Once a horse has learnt to obey, it is easier to deal with, and, in Lily's opinion, the same applies to children:

> "Kids were like horses in that things went a lot easier if you got their respect from the outset rather than trying to demand it after they'd started seeing what they could get away with" (pg. 119).

The other thing that originally appeals to Lily about teaching is being able to work alone and teach in the way that she wants to: "in the classroom, you got to be your own boss" (pg. 57). Most of the time, she works in one-room schools located in remote towns, and has a large amount of freedom with regard to teaching methods and material. This does not always win her the approval of the local residents, for example when she tries to teach Mormon girls about the opportunities of the wider world, she is fired several times. It is also telling that the only time she does not enjoy teaching is when she is working in a large school in Phoenix. Not only does she have to deal with wealthy, disrespectful students, but she is not able to run things her way. Instead, she has to get in line with the other teaching staff and deal with a lot of paperwork: "There were more rules for teachers than for students" (pg. 281).

She likes 'being her own boss'

She does not like teaching in a big school

However, teaching really is her "calling" (pg. 56), and it is not only facts that she wants to get across. She also feels a strong need to impart lessons that can be learnt from life experience, particularly to her own children. This is because she herself has had to learn many things the hard way. Therefore, when such a situation occurs, she is never slow to point it out, especially to Rosemary: "Let that be a lesson to you" (pg. 183) is a phrase we can imagine her using often. These "lessons" range from the importance of protecting domestic animals (the case of Bossie the cow) to not wasting time doing something that won't be properly appreciated (when Lily spends a day and a half making cottage cheese that gets eaten so quickly she feels it was not worth her while making it), and are often connected to learning from the negative consequences of one's actions. From time to time, however, Lily has a more positive life message, for example

Teaching is her 'calling', not only in the classroom

She wants to teach everyone lessons about life

when she and Rosemary are taking her father's body back to the KC Ranch to be buried. Rosemary is very embarrassed by the looks and the comments they get because of the dead body in the back of the car, but Lily takes it in her stride: "Life's too short, honey [...] to worry what other people think of you" (pg. 245). A lot of the time, Lily finds her attempts to teach her daughter about the things she considers important a frustrating experience: Rosemary never seems to want to learn from her, and Lily cannot really understand why. In fact, when Rosemary tells her mother about her engagement, Lily shows her disapproval by saying, "Haven't I taught you anything?" (pg. 319). The trouble is that Lily is convinced that she is always right, but her daughter challenges the idea that Lily knows what is good for her better than she does herself. When it comes to teaching her daughter, Lily is forced to admit defeat:

Lily is frustrated because she doesn't feel she has taught Rosemary anything

> "I always liked to think I'd never met a kid I couldn't teach [...] Turns out I was wrong. That kid is you" (pg. 319).

Lily has little time for ignorant people

When it comes to relationships with other people, Lily often does not have much time for anyone whose opinions she does not share, or who she feels are lacking in some way. Her comments about others are often scathing, especially if she thinks they are rather stupid. For example, her first employer in Chicago, who she refers to as "Mim", is not nearly as intelligent as Lily herself: "In fact, I wondered if anyone could really be such a dodo" (pg. 94). In this case, Lily learns the hard way that showing someone else that you are cleverer than them is not always a good move. Once, she makes the mistake of giving Mim the answer to a crossword clue she is having trouble with, and is fired shortly afterwards. The problem, it seems is her "attitude" (ibid.): Mim tells Lily, "I don't like the way you look at me. [...] A maid should keep her head down" (pg. 95). Her superior intelligence is obviously intimidating, and she discovers that, if she wants to keep a job as a servant, she will have to keep her opinions to herself. This goes against her nature, but she does it in order to make a living.

She learns it is not a good idea to be more intelligent than her employer

Her strong character can cause problems in her relationships with others

Quite often, her relationships with other women are difficult, due to the fact that she is such a strong, self-confident woman. Although these are generally positive characteristics, in Lily's case they make her somewhat insensitive to other people's feelings and personalities. She often cannot put herself in the other person's shoes and see things from their point of view. This can be seen both in her relationship with her mother and, in turn, in her relationship with her daughter. Her mother "didn't quite know what to make of me" (pg. 34), because as a child she is neither particularly good-looking nor at all ladylike, which, as far as Mom is concerned, are both factors that will make it difficult for Lily to find a good husband. She does admire her daughter's courage and ability to get things done, but with reservations: "I never knew a girl to have such gumption [...]. But I'm not too sure that's a good thing" (ibid.). Lily, in turn, does not have a very high opinion of her mother when it comes to being practical, and does not have much time for Mom's ladylike pretensions. For example, whenever Mom faints, which happens quite a lot, Lily does not believe this is a sign that she is ladylike and delicate, but that it happens because her corsets are too tight. Lily sees that the way her mother dresses and behaves is inappropriate for the place where they live and the kind of lifestyle they lead, and is often impatient with this.

Difficult mother-daughter relationships

She has similar problems with her sister Helen, who is like their mother in many ways, including the fact that she is not really suited to life on a ranch. Although Lily clearly loves her sister, which can be seen in her attempts to help her when Helen becomes accidentaly pregnant, she is frustrated by Helen's inability to tackle the problem with some of the practical solutions that she has come up with. If Lily had found herself in the same situation, she would have dealt with it and moved on with her life. She cannot understand why Helen is so unrealistic about the situation, as her reaction is in complete contrast to what Lily's would have been. It is a terrible shock to her when Helen sees suicide as the only way to escape her problems.

She also finds it hard to identify with Helen

It is difficult for Lily to put herself in Helen's position

However, Lily's most conflicted relationship is that with her daughter. This is the relationship in which Lily has the most problems in understanding the other person and seeing things from their point of view. From the

Lily wants to change Rosemary to be more like her

start, Lily expects Rosemary to be like her, with the same priorities and interests. Inevitably, she is often disappointed when this does not happen. Rosemary, for example, hates school and learning, and does not listen to her mother's opinion. Having said this, there are times when they enjoy being together, such as during the wild taxi ride for the three unsuspecting women from New York. In typical style, Lily dismisses the women as "ninnies who wore too much makeup" (pg. 219); nonetheless, they are customers for her taxi service and she takes them out for a drive. When it comes to driving down a long slope, Lily has to drive wildly to keep the car on the road, because the brakes do not work. The Brooklyn women are terrified, and Lily and Rosemary enjoy a laugh at their expense. They are both fearless in situations like these and are united in their scorn for "a bunch of sissies" (pg. 222) who are not used to living wildly. Moreover, they share a love of wide open spaces and the freedom that comes from living there. The difference is that Lily still believes it is important to plan for the future, to be prepared for any disaster that might come along, whereas for Rosemary freedom means complete freedom, not worrying about the future but taking each day as it comes. Lily sees this lack of focus as a character flaw, and, despite Jim's efforts to make her accept her daughter for who she is, never really does so.

At times they get on well

Lily and Rosemary are both fearless

They have different attitudes towards the future

There are, however, some women that Lily admires: Dorothy, Minnie and Mother Albertina. Like her, they are all strong, practical women who get things done and make things happen, so she is able to identify with them. For example, she likes Dorothy because she is able to run the ranch; she also probably saves Dad's life by stopping him from shooting their neighbor. Minnie is the only real female friend that Lily mentions: she is a confident young woman who is not afraid to get what she wants. And, of course, Mother Albertina is the first person to really see Lily's abilities and is the one who puts her on the road to her teaching career. In all of these women, Lily senses a kindred spirit.

She feels an affinity with other strong women

Her relationship with men is often more relaxed, possibly because she is making her way in what was still very much a man's world. Even the teaching profession, although one of the few really open to women at the time, was predominantly male, as she discovers when she loses her first job as an itinerant teacher following the return of the soldiers after the First World War. She seems quite at ease in the masculine world of ranch life, probably because she already did that kind of work as a child. When living in Red Lake the second time, she does not seem to have any female friends, but spends her Saturday evenings with Rooster and his pals, playing poker and drinking whiskey. In a big town, this kind of behavior would almost certainly have been regarded as strange, perhaps inappropriate, but in the small town she is accepted as one of the boys.

She gets on well with men, feeling at ease in a man's world

More male friends than female friends

She gets on well with her father, especially as a child, as they are both tough and thrive in difficult situations. Dad teaches Lily everything he knows; she in turn helps him in many practical ways, managing the ranch and training horses. This is not to say that she admires him unconditionally: she is furious when he spends her school tuition fees on dogs, with the somewhat unrealistic idea of breeding from them. When she is older, she also becomes impatient with him because he still lives in the past and rejects anything that has to do with progress. By now, however, Lily has lived and worked away from the ranch for some time, and sees things from a new perspective. She accepts that he will never change, but knows that she can never go back to living at home.

She has a good relationship with her father but recognizes his faults

Lily and her second husband, Jim, are equals, both in their married life and as business partners. This is the key to their successful relationship, and is vital to Lily after her experience with her first husband, Ted. In general, Lily's attitude to any setbacks she suffers is to cut her losses and carry on: "No looking back" (pg. 267), and this is the way she deals with her failed marriage. However, being married to Ted has left her with a mistrust of men that she never completely gets over, even in her relationship with someone as reliable as Jim. This is why, while they are living in Phoenix, she suspects he may be

She mistrusts men because of her first marriage

having an affair with a co-worker, although this turns out not to be true. Likewise, she is suspicious of Rex's charms, because he reminds her too much of the way she was taken in by Ted. However, she does not succeed in persuading her daughter to look for someone more reliable.

Overall, Lily can be summed up as a strong, intelligent, determined woman who makes the most of life's opportunities. She can be opinionated and intolerant, but is motivated by what she believes in and by a genuine desire to share knowledge with others. When faced with a problem, she can come up with a practical solution. She hates giving up, but if the situation is hopeless she is able to move on without too many regrets. Above all, she is determined never to show weakness. Generally, she doesn't, but there is one occasion when she is so upset at losing her job again that she finds herself crying, without even realizing she is doing so. Instead of, for once, letting her guard down, she becomes angry: "Now, by letting my own daughter see me all weak and pitiful, I felt that I'd failed her in a big way, and I was furious with myself" (pg. 227). She assures Rosemary that she is not crying, but has dust in her eyes: "Because I'm not weak. You'll never have to worry about that" (ibid.). Perhaps she is afraid that, if Rosemary sees her as weak, she will lose respect for her mother, when in fact it might have brought them a little closer together by letting Rosemary see her vulnerable side.

It is important to Lily never to show any signs of weakness

Mom

Mom	
	➙ Lily's delicate, ladylike mother is not really suited to the rough life on the ranch. ➙ Deeply religious and not very practical in everyday matters, one of her biggest concerns is finding a good husband for her two daughters.

Lily's mother, whose maiden name was Daisy Mae Peacock, is someone who seems rather out of place in her surroundings, especially while the family is living in the dugout on Salt Draw. Although her own family did not

Mom is too genteel and delicate for the ranch

live in luxury – they had lived in mining towns – she had been brought up "in an atmosphere of gentility" (pg. 23). As a child, her pale skin had to be protected from the sun, and as an adult she avoids going outside unless it is absolutely necessary. She is determined to be ladylike, despite her circumstances, rubbing a special mixture onto her hands to keep them white and wearing very tight corsets, like Victorian ladies, to make her waist look even smaller than it already was. Because of this, she often faints, which Mom herself considers to be "a sign of her high breeding and delicate nature" (pg. 33). Moreover, Mom tries to pass on her gentility to her children, too, especially to her daughters, by taking good care of their hair and, in Lily's case, buying her a fan to cover her mouth when she laughs, as her teeth stick out. This is part of her campaign to make her daughter more ladylike. As well as this, Mom decorates the dugout with some fine furnishings, her most precious possession being a carved headboard that had belonged to her parents: "[...] it was the only thing that allowed her to sleep at night because it reminded her of the civilized world" (pg. 23).

She is like a Victorian lady

She tries to make their home more civilized

Despite her attempts to make her home comfortable, Mom "hadn't bargained for" (pg. 24) life on Salt Draw, having expected a more comfortable lifestyle since her husband's family were fairly well off in terms of farm land and animals. However, since Lily's father and his siblings had been involved in legal battles over their inheritance since the death of their own father, he had not yet received the expected wealth. Mom is not really a typical rancher's wife, refusing to do any hard physical work, although she does keep the dugout clean and tidy. In addition to this, she has a maid, Lupe, to help her with tasks such as washing and cooking. Her views of the role of men and women are typical of her time: her daughters need to find good husbands and her son will inherit the ranch. However, Mom does admit to Lily that she had been disappointed when she'd had to leave school: "I wanted you to finish your education" (pg. 70). She clearly does not want her daughters to be badly educated, even if she sees schooling as a way to make them more marriageable: later, she also wants to send Helen

She expected a better life for herself

Education for girls is a way to improve their chances of getting a husband to the convent school to give her some "polish" (pg. 89); unfortunately, there is no money available for this.

She is worried about Lily being too manly

However, as Lily is the one doing most of the work around the ranch, Mom relies on her heavily (as she later relies on Dorothy, Buster's wife). She has conflicting feelings about this: on the one hand, she needs Lily to be so practical, but is not sure it is right for her to take on men's work: she believes that men need to feel "manly" (pg. 34) and that Lily is not ladylike enough. Moreover, she is not really keen on Lily working with horses. For one thing, riding a lot makes her "a little bowlegged" (ibid.), which in turn makes her less attractive. As well as this, Mom is frightened that her daughter will end up hurting herself seriously when she is thrown and is horrified when, after Lily has broken her arm quite badly, Dad intends for her to carry on breaking horses.

Mom and Helen are close

It is perhaps not surprising that Mom has a much closer relationship with her daughter Helen than with Lily; she and Helen are similar both in looks and in character. She even thinks it is a good idea for Helen to move to Hollywood, sure that she will either make it as a movie star or find a rich husband, not realizing, of course, that this will end in disaster.

Mom is very religious

Mom is a deeply religious person. In her first appearance in the story, she has been up all night praying for the safe return of her children, and clearly believes that her faith is the reason they survived the night: "You get down on your knees and thank your guardian angel [...]. And you thank me, too" (pg. 16). Buster and Helen follow her lead and pray with her, but Lily sees that it was her own actions that saved them, not her mother's prayers. Mom usually resorts to prayer in times of crisis rather than attempting to do something practical, and is rather fatalistic in her attitude. For her, whatever happens is God's will, and they have to accept it.

After Lily leaves home for good, we do not hear much more about Mom. When Lily gets back from Chicago, Mom is much frailer than before and says her teeth hurt; we later learn that she died from blood poisoning, caused by her teeth.

Dad

	Dad
→ Lily's father is an expert on horses and a good teacher. → He educates Lily at home until she is thirteen, and also teaches her all about horse-breaking. → He is a strong character who does his best to deal with whatever life throws at him. → Lily is similar to him in many ways.	

Dad was disabled by an accident

By his own description, Lily's father, Adam Casey, is a "tough nut" (pg. 17). Physically disabled by an accident at the age of three, when he was kicked in the head by a horse, partly deaf due to working in his family's mill when he was young and with a severe speech impediment, he is not perhaps the kind of person one would expect to be running a ranch. In fact, he would not be able to do it without help, primarily from Lily and their servant Apache. It is possible that Lily gets her love of teaching from him, for she certainly learns a lot from him, even if some of it is biased to his point of view. Dad is the one who encourages her to be interested in science, but history is the most important subject for him. He teaches his children history "with a decidedly west-of-the-Pecos point of view" (pg. 31), i.e. he supports Mexican and Native American rights rather than those of the English settlers. His own father was Irish, another reason for him to side against the English, who he considers "a bunch of pious hypocrites" (ibid.) because they killed so many Indians. According to him, the "[o]nly difference between a traitor and a patriot is your perspective" (ibid.).

He is a good teacher who encourages learning

He is anti-English and sympathetic toward minorities

Legal disputes with his siblings

Because of an inheritance dispute with his siblings, Dad is constantly getting involved in legal battles when Lily is young. His father, Robert Casey, served in the U.S. cavalry when he first arrived in the country, later became a rancher and built up his herd until it was one of the biggest in the Hondo Valley. Robert Casey was murdered, possibly due to a disagreement about eight dollars, and

Dad's hot temper

after his death his children could not agree on how to divide his herd among them. Dad is always convinced that he has been cheated, and often travels to court to fight legal battles, both with his siblings and with other local ranchers. Because of his hot Irish temper, he "usually returned from these trips trembling with rage" (pg. 25). This is partly due to his frustration that most people have difficulty understanding him, and therefore presume that he is stupid. Sometimes he even fires off his pistol as a way of relieving his frustration, although fortunately his does not usually shoot at people. There are two incidents in which he attempts to do so, but is prevented both times from killing someone. In the first incident, he wants to get his gun to shoot at a tinker who had charged him too much money and then made fun of the way he talks; luckily, Lupe hides his guns. In the second incident, described in more detail above, Lily and Dorothy manage to stop him from shooting Old Man Pucket (pg. 64).

He is prevented from shooting people

He writes to politicians about the issues of the day

Despite what many people think, Dad is anything but stupid. His writing is very articulate, and he often writes letters to politicians about things in the world that worry him, such as "industrialization and mechanization" (pg. 30), which, in his opinion, are "destroying the human soul" (ibid.). Later, this attitude makes Lily impatient with him. "All my life I'd been hearing Dad reminiscing about the past and railing against the future" (pg. 90), she comments when he starts talking about his regret that the President of the United States now has cars at the White House instead of horses and carriages.

His passions include spelling reform

Other matters that he is passionate about include Prohibition and, perhaps a little bizarrely, phonetic spelling, "both of which he saw as cures for mankind's tendency toward irrational behavior" (pg. 30). He is in favor of Prohibition because he has seen too much violence caused by drunkenness. The reason he would like to see an end to the inconsistent spelling in English is that he believes anyone who learned the alphabet would be able to read, which in turn would "virtually wipe out illiteracy" (pg. 31). We can see from this that there is logic in his reasoning, and that he wants changes that will benefit people; however, the changes he wishes to make, such as having words spelled the way they are pronounced, are unlikely to come about. Dad firmly believes that everyone and everything needs a "Purpose in Life" (pg. 41) – it is part of his philosophy. In his

Dad's Theory of Purpose

> "Theory of Purpose […] everything in life had a purpose, and unless it achieved that purpose, it was just taking up space on the planet and wasting everyone's time" (pg. 41-42).

He does not buy his children toys so that they won't waste their time playing, but instead encourages them to do things for real. When Lily's appendix bursts after she is hit in the stomach during a baseball game with some local kids, Dad reassures her that losing her appendix does not matter as it has no Purpose. However, she nearly died just because of a baseball game, which was completely pointless according to his philosophy: "If I wanted to risk my life, I should do it for a Purpose" (ibid.). This makes sense to Lily, and she is determined to find out what her Purpose is – she discovers that her purpose is to become a teacher.

Lily is inspired to find her Purpose in life

Dad gives Lily a general education, as well as teaching her to break and ride horses. He teaches her business sense by sending her into town to sell eggs: "It honed my math and taught me the art of negotiation" (pg. 41). He himself, however, is not always successful in his business ventures, as a lot of his ideas for making money turn out to be what Lily calls "harebrained schemes" (pg. 63). For example, at one point he breeds peacocks with the idea of selling them as an elegant pet, only to find there is little demand for them. He spends Lily's tuition money on four Great Danes, only to have them shot dead by his neighbor. He is most successful at what he does best, which is breeding and training carriage horses. When they move to the KC Ranch, he starts working on all kinds of projects instead of concentrating on all the work that needs to be done on the farm. One such project is a biography of the famous outlaw Billy the Kid, who he once met in person as a teenager.

Dad does not have a very good business sense

Dad's money-making schemes

His ideas tend to be impractical

Dad is convinced that this biography will make the family rich, as Westerns are hugely popular. Moreover, the book is intended to "prove that Dad, despite his speech impediment, was better with words than anyone who'd ever laughed at him" (pg. 52). Lily, however, sees these projects as just another example of how Dad was "never the most practical man in the world" (pg. 51), and that it means she will have to take on even more responsibility for the running of the ranch.

Dad relies on Lily – it is hard for him to let her go

Dad relies on Lily far more than on anyone else, and it is difficult for him to see her making her own way in life. He agrees to let her take the teaching test only reluctantly because he needs her on the ranch. In the end, she is able to persuade him by using his own philosophy, i.e. that she has to find her Purpose in life. Faced with this argument, he cannot refuse to let her go. However, he remains convinced that she will only be truly happy living on the ranch: "She'll be back [...] She'll miss ranch life. She's got horse blood in her veins" (pg. 75). Lily stays away for four years and has clearly changed during that time: "You left a girl and you came back a woman" (pg. 88). It is obvious to her that she no longer fits in on the ranch, but Dad finds this hard to accept. His dislike of change makes him believe that everything can now return to the way it was before. He is sure that she will want to go back to working with horses, and cannot understand why she is not really keen: "Don't go talking nonsense. [...] You belong here" (pg. 90). It takes a while, but he does eventually come to realize that Lily has gone for good, and, when she returns home briefly after her years in Chicago, does not expect her to stay. However, when Dad is dying, Lily is the one he turns to when he needs someone to come and fetch him home: "You've always been my best hand" (pg. 242). She cannot refuse, and manages to reach him just before he dies, and to make sure he is buried on his own land, as he has requested.

He finds it hard to accept that Lily does not want to come back to the ranch

He relies on her right up to the end of his life

Buster

	Buster
→ Lily's brother is not the brightest of boys, academically speaking, but is cheerful and charming. → Being the only boy in the family, he is automatically the one who takes over the running of the KC Ranch.	

Buster has a likable personality

We do not learn a great deal about Lily's brother. Two years younger than her, he is the middle child and the only boy. It is therefore clear that he will be the one to take over the ranch from his father. He is not much to look at: "a rabbity little kid" but has an "irresistible smile" (pg. 34) and is very charming: "one of the fastest and smoothest talkers in the county" who could "charm the sage of the brush" (ibid.). Mom adores him and always encourages him to believe he can become whatever he wants, from a successful businessman to the governor of Texas, if that is his dream. However, it is soon clear that he does not have the ambition or motivation for a high-flying career, even though he is sent away to "a fancy Jesuit school" (pg. 53) at the age of ten to give him the good education necessary for his future. Typically for the time, their parents consider it more important for boys to be well educated than girls, which is why, when Dad spends Lily's tuition money on dogs, there is still enough left to keep Buster in school. Lily senses the unfairness here, as she is the one who is really interested in learning, not her brother.

His education is considered more important than his sisters'

Buster leaves school after the eighth grade. His parents would like him to continue his education one day, but he has had enough of school: "He knew enough math and reading and writing to run a ranch, and he didn't see much point in picking up more knowledge than that. Cluttered the mind, in his view" (pg. 72). He and Dorothy, the daughter of the ranch's tenants, fall in love and get married. Dorothy is a strong woman, like Lily in many ways, and is the ideal person to help Buster run the ranch: "He was always a little unmotivated, and if he was going to run the ranch with any success, he'd need someone determined and hardworking like Dorothy beside him" (ibid.). And this is what happens. The two of them turn the ranch into a good business, have a few children, and inherit the KC Ranch when Dad dies.

He doesn't see any point in continuing his schooling

He marries Dorothy and successfully runs the ranch with her help

Helen

Helen	
	➟ Like her mother, Helen is delicate and not suited to rough physical work. ➟ She tries to fulfill her dream of becoming a Hollywood actress, but instead becomes accidentally pregnant and kills herself rather than facing the consequences of giving birth to an illegitimate child.

Helen never goes to school

She seems unmotivated and dislikes physical work

She dreams of becoming an actress

Lily's sister Helen is the youngest child and the one who meets a tragic end. Like Buster, Helen is quite different from Lily, both in looks – she is small, pretty and delicate, like their mother – and in character. Unlike her older siblings, she does not receive any kind of formal education: all she knows she has been taught by her father, through Lily. She is also similar to their mother in that she is not really cut out for life on the ranch. The two of them have a close relationship: "Sometimes they read poetry to each other, and in the stifling midafternoon heat, they'd simply lie together on Mom's chaise longue" (pg. 33). In contrast to Lily, it seems unlikely that Helen will have a career: apart from anything else, she "lacked get-up-and-go" (pg. 89). She does not enjoy physical work that goes beyond baking and sewing, and so is unlikely to make a suitable rancher's wife. Her only real option for the future seems to be marriage to someone in the city, where life would not be physically tough for her. Helen herself dreams of Hollywood stardom, and wants to move to Los Angeles.

Helen is very naive

She does not see that she is being used

Another striking contrast between Lily and her sister is Helen's naivety. She does indeed move to L. A. and works in a milliner's while waiting to get her big break. She remains convinced that it is only a matter of time until she gets a movie role; from her letters, Lily can see what her situation is really like. Clearly, she is being used by a series of men who promise to help her start her movie career, but are only interested in sleeping with her and then moving on to the next would-be actress. Helen does not see anything wrong with this, but believes that "this was the way all girls made it in Hollywood" (pg. 130). After a while, the inevitable happens: Helen becomes accidentaly pregnant and is abandoned by the baby's father. Interestingly, it is Lily she turns to in this crisis, too ashamed to contact her parents and unable to find a solution to the problem herself. Lily does her best to help, inviting Helen to come and stay and suggesting several different options that do not involve a backstreet abortion. All of Lily's suggestions are typically practical, but Helen is not the practical type, and does not seem able to seriously consider any of them, instead focusing on "totally ludicrous plans and pointless concerns" (pg. 132). After a while, it seems that Helen will never manage to make a decision, although the need to do so is becoming more urgent every day, especially once her pregnancy becomes public knowledge. When Lily is threatened with being fired unless Helen leaves, she once again tries to persuade her sister to return to the KC Ranch, sure that their parents will understand and take her in. However, Helen does not believe her, sure that she will be disowned by her parents and have nowhere to go. She has more or less given up hope, but Lily has not, and carries on trying to make her sister see the positive side. After a while, it seems as if she has succeeded: "'Maybe you're right,' [Helen] said. 'Maybe there's a way'" (pg. 138). What Lily does not suspect at that moment is that Helen's way of dealing with her problems will be to kill herself. This tragedy affects Lily deeply.

She is ashamed to return home to her parents

She is unable to decide what to do about her pregnancy

Her solution is suicide

Ted Conover

Ted Conover	
→ Lily's first husband is charming and fun to be with at first. → However, it turns out that their whole marriage is a lie, as he already has a wife and family in another part of the city.	

Lily meets Ted Conover at a time in her life when she is extremely vulnerable. Her best friend, Minnie, has just been tragically killed, she is alone in a big city, thousands of miles from her family, doing a job she dislikes. Add to this the fact that she is inexperienced anyway when it comes to men and it is easy to see why she falls for his charms. She is not completely naive – she sees that his

Lily falls for Ted because she is vulnerable

methods for selling vacuum cleaners are rather aggressive and perhaps not quite honest – but, because he has "the gift of [the] gab" (pg. 98) he is easy to talk to, and makes her laugh. In addition to this, he takes her out for meals and to sporting events, treats her to champagne and even teaches her to swim. "You'll have to trust me" (pg. 100) he says, while teaching her, and she does. It doesn't take long for her to fall in love with him.

He treats her well at first

They get married only a couple of months after they first meet, and move into a boardinghouse for married couples. In some ways, Ted seems ideal for Lily: she is used to hard work, and does not like spending money on what she considers to be unnecessary items, whereas he enjoys life and likes to have fun, encouraging Lily to do the same. He also makes her feel that her dreams and ambitions are important: "Ted always encouraged people to think big, to dream big" (pg. 102). She should not just go to college, but should get a Ph. D. while she's there; not only should she learn to fly a plane, she should become a stunt pilot. She is swept away by his enthusiasm, and accepts his story that he is a traveling salesman who has to work away from Chicago a lot.

Ted encourages Lily to enjoy life more

His enthusiasm inspires her

It therefore comes as a severe shock when she finds out the truth about Ted: that he has a wife and family in another part of the city. As well as this, she discovers he has taken most of the money they had saved up together, a terrible blow for her as she has worked so hard to save money for their future. When she confronts him, attacking him physically in her anger, he at first threatens to hit her back if she does not calm down. Lily, however, does not allow herself to be intimidated by him. She demands to know why he ever courted her in the first place when he was already married. Even now, he attempts to play on her feelings, claiming that he loves her, but Lily will have none of it: "The louse was acting as if he expected me to feel sorry for him" (pg. 108). She has finally seen through him and, although she is very upset about what has happened, she is able to cut her losses and start again. The one lasting effect of their relationship is that Lily no longer entirely trusts men, and quite often automatically assumes the worst, especially

He turns out to be a bigamist who has stolen her money

Even after his cover has been blown, he tries to play on her feelings if they remind her of Ted in any way. For example, Ted is one reason why she never really accepts Rex Walls as being good enough to marry her daughter.

Jim Smith

→ Lily's second husband is steady and reliable. → Although he is nearly twenty years older than her, they have a lot in common and stay together through good times and bad.	Jim Smith

Lily first meets Jim Smith during her second stay in Red Lake, when he is judging a horse race she is taking part in. They become friends, and before long it is clear to Lily that Jim would like something more than friendship, but he does not pressure her in any way, or even talk to her about the possibility of their becoming a couple. In fact, it is Lily who decides that they should get married, following the death of her sister. Before that, she was sure that she did not want to get married again after her experience with her "previous crumb-bum husband" (pg. 127); however, she comes to see that Jim is a completely different kind of person to Ted Conover. One point in his favor is that he doesn't talk needlessly all the time, but he "spoke when he had something to say, and if he didn't, he felt no need to fill the void with hot air" (ibid.). This is a contrast to Ted, for whom smooth talking was part of his job, and also part of the tactics he used to attract Lily.

Jim and Lily are friends long before they get married

Jim does not talk unless it is necessary

This is not the only difference between Jim and Lily's ex-husband. Although he led an adventurous life as a young man, working, among other things, as a lumberjack, a homesteader and a prospector, Jim is now a reliable businessman, running a successful garage. In addition to this, he has a strong connection to animals and nature: he is an excellent horseman and, as the incident with the lambs and ewes demonstrates, knows how to deal with animals and solve problems calmly: he is good in a crisis. Another example is his ability to recognize the signs that show a hard winter is coming, as he does when the family is living in Phoenix. It seems only

Jim is experienced and reliable

He is good in a crisis

natural that he is the one the authorities turn to for advice and practical help during that particular winter outbreak: his skill and experience save many ranchers' livelihoods. However, the most important quality for Lily when deciding that Jim is the man she wants to spend her life with is that she feels she can trust him. Later, when they are living in Phoenix, she becomes uncertain about this for a while, and starts to think that maybe she cannot trust him completely after all, that maybe he is having an affair with a co-worker. When Jim finds out that Lily has been spying on him, he does not become angry at her lack of trust in him, but shows that he understands why she thought he might be cheating on her. He sees it as a sign that city life is not good for them, and agrees to move away from Phoenix and the bad atmosphere it has created between them.

He is trustworthy

Jim understands why Lily thinks he may be having an affair

There are a lot of other things about Jim's personality that appeal to Lily. He is a very calm person: "nothing ever rattled Jim Smith" (pg. 129) and he "never lost his temper" (ibid.). He is extremely observant, both of things that can be seen physically, such as someone riding a horse in the distance or an eagle's nest high up on a cliff, but also of people, which enables him to assess their character accurately: "He could spot liars, cheaters, and bluffers from the get-go" (ibid.). However, he keeps his opinion of other people to himself: "while nothing escaped him, he never let on that he knew what he knew" (ibid.). He does not judge others: for example, he is not against the sale of bootleg liquor during Prohibition, even though he himself no longer drinks, believing that people should be able to have a drink if they want one. This is why he agrees to let Mr. Lee hide his illegal alcohol in their house. The only reason he does not want Lily to sell it is that he does not want her to get caught and possibly be sent to prison.

He is a good judge of character

He is non-judgemental

He and Lily are similar in many ways. For one thing, they are not afraid of hard work: "Jim and I both knew how to roll up our sleeves" (pg. 169). They like the outdoor life and do not mind living in small towns or on remote ranches, preferring them to big cities like Phoenix. They are practical people, who are able to come up with solutions to their problems. For example, on their first ranch, they realize that they need some

Jim and Lily do not mind hard work

They are good at finding practical solutions

way of trapping rain water for use throughout the year, and come up with the idea of hiring a bulldozer to dig out some dams. Later, when extremely heavy rainfalls threaten to destroy the dams, Jim gets the whole family to help him save them by attaching a plow to the back of their pickup. They both have a good head for business, which helps their ranch to survive the Depression at a time when others are going bankrupt. One reason they manage this is by being "frugal" (pg. 200): doing as many jobs as possible themselves, reusing everything they can and not spending money on any non-essentials, going as far as to drink from old coffee cans instead of cups.

He gives Lily the freedom to realize her dreams

Jim and Lily really are "partners" (pg. 146) in their marriage. He treats his wife as an equal in business matters, and does not stand in the way of her ambitions, for example when she wants to learn to fly a plane. He gives her the freedom to be herself. On the other hand, he is not afraid to step in if he feels she is in danger, such as when he makes her stop selling the bootleg alcohol, or if he thinks something is unfair, such as when he forbids her to play poker with their ranch hands, whose money she keeps winning. Most of all, Jim accepts Lily for the person she is. For example, when she loses yet another teaching job, this time because she has beaten the local deputy's son, he is not terribly surprised: "'This is getting almost predictable', he said. [...] 'These showdowns. It's becoming a pattern'" (pg. 226). He understands that it is part of her personality that she will not allow herself to be "pushed around" (ibid.), but will stand up for what she believes, and he does not try to change her, or to tell her to modify her behavior so that she will keep her job.

He does not try to change who she is

One thing that is important to Jim is to feel useful, that he is not wasting his talents. It is very hard for him when the ranch is sold to the rich Hollywood director and he is told he will not be needed any more, mainly because he does not fit in with the new owner's idea of what a cowboy should look like. This makes him feel like an animal that is no longer able to do any useful work: "Guess I've been put out to pasture" (pg. 266). After this incident, he is not really happy again until the

He needs to feel useful

Arizona Department of Agriculture calls on him to help out during the crisis caused by the snowstorm. Although it involves a lot of hard, physical work and doing dangerous things like parachuting out of planes, he is given a sense of purpose once more, and returns home exhausted but happy. This is why he could never be satisfied for long with a desk job, and why everything is much better when the family moves away from the big city and back to a small town where he is once again able to work with his hands.

He is not really happy unless he is working with his hands

Jim has a good relationship with his daughter. They enjoy each other's company, although they are quite different in character. Jim is calm and steady while Rosemary has a "wild streak" (pg. 181), but in their case it seems that opposites attract: "They were happy to spend hours in each other's company, Rosemary talking nonstop and Jim barely saying a word, just nodding and smiling" (ibid.). Later, when Rosemary tells her parents that she and Rex are going to get married, Jim is not upset about it in the way that Lily is: "Jim was philosophical about Rosemary's decision, figuring that since her mind was made up, we'd only turn her against us by arguing with her" (pg. 320). He does not really approve of Rex, either, thinking that he talks too much but without there being much substance behind what he says: "If we could harness the hot air coming out of that gasbag [...] we could power the whole of Phoenix" (pg. 305). Unlike Lily, he does not try to change his daughter, but accepts her for who she is. He understands that she is a free spirit who would not be happy living a conventional lifestyle. He is able to let go, and encourages Lily to do the same.

Jim gets on well with Rosemary and accepts her for who she is

Rosemary

Rosemary	➟ Lily's artistic daughter does not always see eye to eye with her mother – being very different types of people, they often disagree. ➟ In the end, despite her mother's disapproval, Rosemary goes her own way.

Rosemary's relationship with her mother is a difficult one because the two of them have such different personalities. In many ways, Rosemary is the opposite of Lily. Even as a young child, she often does not do what Lily wants and expects of her. For example, Lily thinks it is very important for her to take on responsibility on the ranch from a young age, but Rosemary finds the everyday jobs that have to be done boring. Her father does not see this is as a problem because Rosemary is still so young, but Lily is afraid that if her daughter does not concentrate on the important things in life right from the start, she never will: "I began to worry that Rosemary was unfocused and that if we didn't stamp it out early, it could become a permanent part of her character" (pg. 184). This shows how Lily does her best to shape Rosemary's character, to turn her daughter into the person she, Lily, thinks she should be. Right from the start, Rosemary resists this and does what she wants to do.

Lily wants Rosemary to take on responsibility, even as a young child

Rosemary does not want to be like her mother

Even as a baby, Rosemary is beautiful. She reminds Lily of her sister Helen, but not in a good way: "Helen's beauty, as far as I was concerned, had been a curse, and I resolved that I would never tell Rosemary she was beautiful" (pg. 153). As Rosemary gets older, Lily becomes more aware of the dangers that might arise from her daughter's good looks, and makes sure she is never alone with any of the cowboys on their ranch. By the time she is thirteen, she is "quite a looker" (pg. 250) although, to her mother's relief, she herself seems unaware of this. Of course, this does not mean that others do not notice her: Fidel Hanna, the young ranch hand, is clearly as attracted to her as she is to him, which gets her into trouble during the visit of the two education department inspectors. First of all, she rides down to the Havasupai village with him on his horse, leaving her mother and the other white women behind. The two inspectors in particular disapprove of this wild behavior, and Lily is afraid they will think she has not brought her daughter up properly. Then, one evening, Rosemary sneaks out of the room to go swimming in her underwear with Fidel and some other Havasupai boys. This is the last straw for Lily. Not only has Rosemary deliberately disobeyed her,

Lily is worried that Rosemary's good looks might lead to trouble

Her behavior is wild and inappropriate for a white girl

She deliberately disobeys her mother

but, despite her mother's warnings, has put herself in a potentially dangerous situation. She has chosen to ignore what her mother told her, that "seemingly innocent situations could result in trouble, that one misstep could lead to a disaster she might never recover from" (pg. 260). Lily is clearly thinking of Helen here, whose good looks did get her into terrible trouble. Rosemary seems like a fairly typical teenager here, rebelling against the rules she has been told to follow. After this incident, Rosemary is sent away to boarding school again in an attempt to keep her out of trouble.

Lily tries to find her an alternate career to stop her from becoming an artist

There is just one time that Lily tries to use Rosemary's beauty to her advantage. Wondering what kind of career her daughter might have, Lily thinks that she might be able to become a model or a beauty queen. However, although she looks the part, Rosemary "moved like a cowgirl, not a beauty queen" (pg. 279), lacking the elegance that a model needs. Lily pays for some modeling lessons, but even after she has learnt to move like a model, Rosemary is unable to relax in front of a camera, and it becomes clear that this is not the right career for her.

They share a love of nature

However, Rosemary and Lily do have some things in common. For one thing, they both love nature and the outdoor life. Rosemary is a "tomboy" (pg. 250) who loves to run wild. Lily compares her to a half-broke horse:

> "She was happiest running around out of doors, without a stitch of clothing if I'd let her. She climbed the cedar trees, splashed in the horse trough, peed in the yard, swung from vines, and jumped from the barn rafters onto the hay bales" (pg. 178).

She loves galloping around on horses, and even when she is older she "always had to have the most spirited horse in the herd" (pg. 307). Away from the countryside, Rosemary feels trapped, both when she is sent away to school and when the family is living in Phoenix – she misses the freedom of the wide open spaces and cannot settle in a city. She "hated the black asphalt and the gray concrete. [...] Phoenix was square and straight, boxy and boxed in, and above all, fake" (pg. 273). She is not really happy again until they leave Phoenix and move to the very remote village of Horse Mesa.

She hates living in a city

Rosemary loves animals, and she "hated to see any animal caged, tied up, or penned in" (pg. 179), preferring to let them run free, even if this does mean, for example, that their chickens might get eaten by a wild animal. She finds it hard to accept that keeping animals fenced in is necessary on a ranch, both to protect the animals themselves and to protect the rancher's livelihood. In contrast, Lily is not sentimental about animals. For her, they serve a purpose: horses are for riding, traveling and working on the ranch. Cattle are raised to be sold and slaughtered for food – this is how they make their living. Even Bossie, the beautiful, expensive Guernsey cow they are given, is kept for practical reasons: to give good milk and to breed from, bringing more money to the ranch. Rosemary learns a hard lesson when she tries to give Bossie her freedom and the cow dies through overeating. She has to accept that domestic animals, at least, are kept shut up for a reason. Later, when she is older, she tries to come to terms with the realities of life as a rancher, for example by taking part in the skinning of a steer. Although she sees the job through to the end, she is clearly upset by it, and it becomes obvious that she will never see animals simply as a source of food and money. Both she and her parents have to accept that life as a rancher is not for her.

Rosemary loves all animals and wants them to be free

Her love of animals is in conflict with the realities of ranch life

When it comes to education, Rosemary also fails to live up to her mother's expectations. From the age of three, Lily tries to teach her math and reading, but Rosemary does not show as much interest as Lily would like. Later, when she is sent away to school, she shows a similar lack of commitment to learning. At both schools she attends, she is very homesick, and does not fit in with the other girls. She appears wild and badly behaved because she has not had the same genteel upbringing as the others. In addition to this, she does not enjoy the more ladylike aspects of her education: she "found embroidery and etiquette excruciating" (pg. 238). It seems that she can do nothing right: "She sang too loudly, she danced too enthusiastically, she spoke out of turn, she drew whimsical pictures in the margins of her books" (ibid.). Often, the things she says are considered "inappropriate" (ibid.), although much of the time she is sim-

Rosemary shows a lack of interest in learning

Her wild behavior at school makes her an outsider

ply repeating Lily's opinions or reflecting her attitude to certain things. Because she is so different, she gets teased a lot by the other girls, but she is not afraid to defend herself. For example, when one of the girls makes fun of her 'cowboy' father, saying that Rosemary thinks he is John Wayne, Rosemary's response is "My dad makes John Wayne look like a pussy" (pg. 239), after which she "dunked the girl's head in the dishwater" (ibid.). Lily is proud of Rosemary for standing up for herself: "Maybe she's got a bit of her mother in her after all" (ibid.). Clearly, this is true: Rosemary is like Lily in that she has a strong personality; it is just that her goals in life are quite different to her mother's. She does not do well academically at either of the schools she goes to, not because she lacks intelligence, but because boarding school does not suit her personality.

She can stand up for herself

Rosemary is very artistic, and, from a young age, shows a lot of talent for drawing and painting. When they are living on the Hackberry ranch, she has no trouble creating "perfect little line drawings without once lifting the pencil off the paper" (pg. 199). Later, Rosemary's ambition is to become an artist, which Lily does not think is a good or secure career choice. However, eventually Rosemary is allowed to take drawing lessons with a French art teacher, who teaches her how to look at the world in a different way and discover all the beauty in it. These are the kinds of ideas that appeal to Rosemary. She feels that the best thing about painting is that "If there's something about the world that you don't like, you can paint a painting that makes it the way you want it to be" (pg. 280). It is at this point that she starts to sign her name "Rose Mary" as she thinks it looks nicer. At university, she is allowed to study art, but on the condition that this remains a sideline: she also has to get her teaching certificate. Rosemary is not entirely happy about this: she "still thought I was imposing my will on her" (pg. 301), but accepts the compromise. It is clear, however, that her art is more important to her than anything else. In fact, one of the things that attracts her to Rex is that he likes her paintings and takes her seriously as an artist, something that her mother does not do. In fact, Lily does not even have any of her daughter's

She is artistic and wants to make her living as an artist

Lily tries to discourage her artistic ambitions

Rex likes her art

pictures displayed in their home, because "they don't match the rug" (pg. 304). Rex, however, loves her work, calling her paintings "goddamned masterpieces" (ibid.). After she marries Rex, Rosemary continues "painting like a fiend" (pg. 325), as well as taking care of all the children she starts to have.

Rosemary is very sensitive

Although she is quite wild in some ways, Rosemary is also a sensitive person, which perhaps reflects the artistic side of her personality. As we have seen, she dislikes the idea of killing animals for food, although this does not stop her eating meat: "the girl had a real gift for pushing unpleasantness out of her mind, and that night she tucked into her steak with gusto" (pg. 253) – this is after she has helped to skin the steer. When the family moves to Phoenix, the Second World War is coming to an end, but people are worried by the threat of bombs, so the city's air-raid siren is tested once a week. Rosemary hates and is frightened by the noise it makes. When the atom bomb is dropped on Hiroshima, she is distraught about all the people, mainly civilians, and animals that have been killed, down to the smallest living creatures. For Lily, the situation is an example of the ends justifying the means: it was necessary to end the war somehow to prevent more American soldiers from being killed. Rosemary simply cannot see it from this point of view: "The deaths of all those mice and birds was just as upsetting to her as the deaths of the people. After all, she said, the animals hadn't started the war" (pg. 277). At the Catholic school that she now attends, the nuns show newsreels of the aftermath of the bombs in Hiroshima and Nagasaki, encouraging the students to pray for the Japanese. Lily has little sympathy for this point of view, but the bombing of Japan has a deep effect on her daughter. Although she stops talking about what happened, she expresses her feelings through her artwork. One day Lily finds "a folder full of drawing after drawing of animals and children, all with Japanese eyes and angels' wings" (pg. 278).

She is very upset by the effects of the atom bomb

She expresses her feelings through her art

For Lily, Rosemary's choice of husband is another act of rebellion. Lily is convinced that her daughter needs a "solid" (pg. 301) man, one who is like her father, who will

Rosemary and Lily have different ideas about what kind of man she should marry

encourage her to settle down, become a teacher and lead a steady, conventional life. But this is not the kind of life that Rosemary wants to lead, and she is unlikely to be attracted to a man like that. She is popular with men and gets asked out on lots of dates; many of the men who are attracted to her even propose to her. But Rex Walls is the one she chooses. He is lively, fun to be with, always talking about his plans and ideas for the future. Above all, he takes Rosemary seriously and makes her feel valued.

She has no illusions about Rex but does not want to plan her future down to the last detail

Rosemary wants adventure rather than security

She does not want to be like her mother

Being with Rex is always exciting, and this is what she wants. She knows that he is unreliable and that he won't give her the security her mother wants for her, but feels it is better to live in the present than to spend too much time worrying about the future, as nobody can tell what is going to happen. Lily, who has spent much of her life planning for and working towards her future, cannot understand this attitude at all: "And people who don't plan for the future get ambushed by it. Hope for the best but plan for the worst, my dad always used to say" (pg. 313). However, this argument is not enough to convince Rosemary: "You can't prepare for everything that life's going to throw at you [...]. And you can't avoid danger. It's there. The world is a dangerous place, and if you sit around wringing your hands about it, you'll miss out on all the adventure" (ibid.). This sums up Rosemary's attitude to life very well, and Lily realizes that she will never make her daughter see things from her point of view. In fact, it is partly Lily's determination to change Rosemary's character that has made her daughter the way she is: "That's all you've been doing my whole life. 'Let this be a lesson.' 'Let that be a lesson.' But all these years, what you thought you were teaching me was one thing, and what I was learning was something else" (pg. 319). What Lily has taught Rosemary is that she does not want to be like her mother, that she will follow her own instincts without be tied down by her mother's expectations. Like the wild animals she loves, Rosemary needs to be able to "roam free" (pg. 320). She is a half-broke horse that Lily never manages to tame.

Little Jim

→ Lily's son also loves the outdoor life on the ranch. → He does not cause her as much trouble as Rosemary, and ends up with a good job and a stable marriage.	Little Jim

Little Jim also loves the outdoor life

Like Buster, Little Jim does not feature very prominently in Lily's story. In many ways, he is similar to his sister. He, too, loves living on the ranch and the freedom of the outdoor lifestyle. One of the things he loves most are the huge storms that hit the region during the rainy season. Because there is so little water where they live, a rainstorm is always a special occasion – Little Jim and Rosemary love to go out in the rain, swim and play in the puddles.

He and his sister are good friends

Living on a remote ranch, there are not many opportunities for Little Jim and Rosemary to make friends, and Lily does not encourage this anyway, but the two of them are happy with just each other to play with. They make toys out of junk they find around the ranch and spend their days outside, creating their own adventures.

They love riding horses

Both of them love horse riding, having learnt to ride before they could even walk. One of their favorite activities is to race the train that crosses part of the ranch every afternoon: "they'd gallop alongside it, the passengers leaning out and waving and the engineer sounding the whistle until the train inevitably pulled ahead" (pg. 234). They love the excitement of the race and don't mind that the train beats them every time. Although they live a rough-and-tumble lifestyle, their parents encourage them to be tough and not start crying when they hurt themselves. Sometimes their adventures go a little too far: Little Jim nearly drowns in a sinkhole in their pond, but luckily his father rescues him in time.

He is also similar to Buster in that he is not particularly academic. When attending his mother's school, he often plays her up, causing her to give him "his share of paddlings" (pg. 215). However, being spanked in front of his fellow students does not have much effect on Little Jim. When he is sent away to boarding school, he enjoys it

Little Jim does not like school and frequently tries to escape

even less, and often tries to run away: "climbing over fences and through windows, pulling out nails when the windows were nailed shut, and using tied-together bedsheets to shimmy down from upper floors" (pg. 238). His teachers call him "Little Houdini" (ibid.), but his wild behavior does not really get him into trouble, as his school is used to dealing with ranch boys like him. Academically, Little Jim does not do well at school, and is delighted when Lily takes him and his sister back to live on the ranch. He and Rosemary are "so happy to be home that they ran around hugging everything – cowboys, horses, trees" (pg. 240).

Like the rest of the family, he hates the big city

When the Hackberry ranch is sold and the family has to move away, Little Jim is distraught, saying he will not leave, but of course he has no choice in the matter. When he wants to look back as they drive away for the last time, Lily tells him not to, her attitude being that there is no use in living in the past. Right from the start, he hates living in a big city: "You feel penned in [...]. You feel puny" (pg. 273).

He drops out of university and becomes a policeman

Later, Little Jim starts to study at Arizona State University, but drops out before he has even completed his first year there: "he'd never been much of a student" (pg. 301). Instead, he gets married and becomes a policeman. By this time, the name 'Little Jim' no longer suits him, as he is taller and heavier than his father, and is a college football player. He ends up living in the suburbs of Phoenix with his wife, Diane, and their children.

Rex Walls

Rex Walls	
	➟ Lily does not approve of her son-in-law – although he is charming, he is wild, arrogant and unreliable. ➟ However, he is just the kind of man that Rosemary finds attractive, as his adventurous nature suits her personality. ➟ They get married and set off on a life of adventure together.

Rex is daring but can be aggressive

Rosemary meets Rex Walls one summer at a canyon where she has gone to swim with some friends. He is an air force pilot, or a 'flyboy', and right from the start he is different from the other young men she knows. He tells her the very first time he meets her that they are going to get married, as if it is a certain fact. He certainly makes a striking first impression on Rosemary: "One thing about him – he wasn't a very good swimmer, but he jumped right in" (pg. 302). She likes the fact that he is daring and adventurous. On their very first date, he gets into a fight with another man who flirted with her. The fight gets out of hand, but he and Rosemary managed to run away from the restaurant before the police turned up. Rosemary finds the whole incident very funny – his behavior appeals to the wild side of her character.

He can be very charming

At his first meeting with Rosemary's parents, Rex shows his charming side: "He had courtly manners, sweeping off his air force cap, shaking Jim's hand vigorously, and giving mine a gentle squeeze. 'Now I see where Rosemary gets her looks', he told me" (pg. 303). Lily has to admit that he has charisma: "This fellow did have a way about him" (ibid.) and she is also impressed by the fact he is able to laugh about a serious car accident he had when he was seventeen: "you knew anyone who could laugh off a car accident that took out all his teeth had to have a little gumption" (ibid.). She can understand why Rosemary is attracted to him. Generally, however, she thinks she can see through his charming manner, believing that, although he is fun to be with, he is unreliable and untrustworthy:

Lily does not trust him and thinks he is unreliable

> "This Rex fellow always had a joke on hand, could talk about any subject, passed out compliments like candy, and made you feel you were the center of the world, but you couldn't trust him any further than you could throw him" (pg. 305).

Jim, too, sees Rex as someone who talks a lot without there being very much substance behind what he says. Rosemary, on the other hand, loves his enthusiasm, for example for her art. Moreover, she likes his unconventional behavior, the way that "when he was around, things always happened" (ibid.). He loves talking to strangers, playing tricks and surprising people, such as when he secretly hangs one of Rosemary's paintings in an art museum in Phoenix and takes her to see it. He is not the kind of person who plans ahead, but is someone who "loved to act on whims" (ibid.). Rex is able to turn anything into an adventure, and instinctively recognizes people who are wild like him. These are the kinds of people he most enjoys spending time with, and he takes Rosemary with him on some of his adventures: "You'd go to a circus and meet the clowns, the bareback rider, and the sword swallower, wind up after the show tossing back shots in a bar with all of them, the sword swallower showing you how to stick a knife down your throat" (pg. 306). Rosemary enjoys this as much as he does, even though some of the incidents were "strange, [...] some were exciting, some were funny, some were scary" (ibid.).

He is unconventional and spontaneous

He is an exciting person to be with

Rex is someone who refuses to be beaten once he has made up his mind to do something. One example of this is his determination to marry Rosemary. Another is his desire to learn to ride a horse. The problem is that, as well as being determined, he is rather arrogant, and is sure that he won't have any problems with riding: "I gotta show you all that even though I've never been astride a horse, I got what it takes to ride one" (pg. 307). He does not really listen to Lily's instructions as he is too busy trying to prove that riding a horse is easy for him and that he is ready to gallop, even though he does not know what he is doing: "Instead of relaxing, Rex kept up a steady patter about what a cinch this riding business was, what a blast he was having, and how he wanted to put this old nag through her paces" (pg. 308). Unsurprisingly, he comes to grief, falling off the horse, and is quite shaken at first by the experience. However, he is not afraid to get back on the horse and try again: his determination wins through.

He is determined and does not like giving up

It is not long before Lily and Jim discover a more unpleasant side to Rex's character. Rex likes playing poker and, even more, likes to drink. Being an experienced poker player herself, Lily knows that the way someone plays the game is a good indication of their character. In Rex's case, she sees that he is someone for whom "the game was not about reading your cards, it was about reading your opponents" (pg. 310); in other words, he is a pretty good judge of character himself. Rex's problem, however, is his drinking. The more whiskey he drinks, the more overconfident and arrogant he becomes: "he started playing too grandly, overbluffing, overbetting, losing pots he should never have tried to win" (ibid.). The more he loses, the angrier he becomes, and the more he drinks. Lily takes the opportunity to finish off the game, winning all of his money. At first he laughs it off, being very cheeky to Lily in the process, but when he is about to leave it becomes clear that the alcohol has made him rather aggressive, as he reacts very angrily to the suggestion that he should sleep at their house rather than drive home. He himself admits that this state of affairs is not unusual for him: "I drive like this all the time" (pg. 311), and not even Rosemary can persuade him to stay once he's made up his mind. He would rather put his life in danger than take orders from someone else.

He drinks a lot and becomes aggressive when drunk

Rex does not like being told what to do

Lily is able to experience Rex's daring nature for herself when he takes her flying. Reluctantly, she has to admit that there are some similarities between the two of them: they both like driving fast, they both like flying, and, in the past, they both sold illegal alcohol. They find that they have plenty to talk about and get on well. In the air, after letting Lily fly for a while, Rex carries out several potentially dangerous maneuvers, such as looping the loop and flying very close to the ground. Lily enjoys the thrill of the ride, although she is very much aware of the danger, which is why she calls him "crazy" (pg. 318).

Lily finds they have some things in common when Rex takes her flying

Despite coming to understand more about his background, however, Lily remains convinced that he is not the right man for Rosemary, partly because they are too similar. In her opinion, Rosemary needs someone to give her security, something that Rex will certainly not provide. She thinks his plans for the future are "half-baked" (pg. 319). Neither he nor Rosemary have any specific ideas about where they are going to live or what they are going to live from. In particular, Lily cannot understand that Rosemary does not seem to care where she and her future husband will live: "What do you

Lily knows he will not give Rosemary any security in life

mean, it doesn't matter? The place where you live – your home – is one of the most important things in a body's life" (ibid.). Rosemary does not care about this, and is happy to go wherever life with Rex takes her: "Maybe we'll never settle down" (ibid.). It is clear that this is the way they are going to live right from the start: Rex's plan for their honeymoon is to simply get in the car and drive, without any particular destination in mind, and take in any adventures they might come across. After a typically noisy, fun-filled wedding, the two of them do just that. As they are driving away, Lily realizes that they are both like half-broke horses – they will probably never be tamed. Their married life seems to confirm this: Rex does not really support his family, but just makes a little cash with occasional jobs while working on some of his unrealistic plans to make cash: "machines to mine gold and giant panels to harness the sun's energy" (pg. 325). Whenever they come to visit, Lily and Rex always end up shouting at each other, sometimes nearly getting into a physical fight. It is clear that the two of them will always disagree, but this does not stop Lily staying involved in their lives.

Rex and Rosemary's life together will always be unconventional

Rex and Lily never really get along

Mother Albertina

Mother Albertina	➟ The nun plays an important part in Lily's life, setting her on the path towards becoming a teacher and showing her the importance of never giving up.

Mother Albertina is the principal of the school Lily attends in Santa Fe, The Sisters of Loretto Academy of Our Lady of the Light. She is an important influence in Lily's life, as she is the one who sets Lily on the path towards becoming a teacher. Mother Albertina is a sympathetic character who is always fair and earns the respect of her students: "She was firm without being stern, never raised her voice or lost her temper, but it would have been unthinkable for any of us to disobey her" (pg. 54). Although she is a nun, she has a very modern, almost feminist attitude with regard to a woman's place in society. Many of the girls at her school have been sent there

Mother Albertina influences Lily

She has a modern way of thinking about the role of women

to learn certain social skills and graces to give them a better chance of finding a husband. However, when talking to Lily about her future, Mother Albertina tells her: "But you don't have to get married, you know" (pg 55). This is an unusual attitude for the time, when women were expected to get married rather than have a career. Furthermore, Mother Albertina believes in the importance of women having a back-up plan, of gaining useful skills beyond those needed to be a housewife: "Even women who got married should be capable of doing something, since men had such a habit of dying on you and, from time to time, running off" (pg. 56). She tells Lily that she would make an ideal teacher, recognizing in her the strong character that she herself possesses.

She emphasizes the importance of not relying on a man for security

When Lily has to leave school because her father can no longer pay the fees, Mother Albertina does not allow her to get upset about it: "You're luckier than most girls here – God gave you the wherewithal to handle setbacks like this" (pg. 59). Her attitude reflects one that Lily often shows later in life: do not waste time regretting what might have been, but make the best of things and move on. She does not forget about Lily once she has left the school, but writes to her about the opportunity to take the test that will be the start of her teaching career. Overall, Mother Albertina is a positive role model in Lily's life.

She encourages Lily to have no regrets, but to always look out for future opportunities

Minnie

Minnie
➟ Lily's happy, outgoing friend knows how to enjoy life. ➟ This makes her sudden death all the more tragic.

Minnie Hanagan lives in the same boardinghouse as Lily when she first moves to Chicago and becomes the first real friend Lily has ever had. Minnie is Irish, very beautiful to look at with her green eyes and long black hair. She loves to talk: "Minnie never met a topic she didn't have an opinion on or heard a comment she couldn't interrupt" (pg. 95). She even gets her first taste of politics by going to a few suffragette rallies with Minnie. But

Minnie is lively, attractive and a great talker

what Lily likes most about her is that she can really talk to her about anything and everything, which is a great contrast to her job as a maid, where she is expected to keep her mouth shut and speak only when she is spoken to.

She makes the most of her situation in life

Minnie believes in making the most of what she has, even though she does not have much. When it is Lily's birthday, Minnie gives her a lipstick as a present, and insists that they get dressed up and go to a department store in the city "where we'd have fun trying on all the things we'd be able to buy one of these days" (pg. 96). Lily is slightly nervous in the shop, knowing that she does not have any money, but this does not stop Minnie. The salesclerk, seeing that they are not going to buy anything, would prefer them to leave; Minnie tells her they are leaving because they cannot find anything stylish enough, not because they cannot afford the clothes. She is full of self-confidence: "When they get high-handed, all you have to do is remind yourself that they're just hired help" (ibid.) and does not feel inferior to anyone.

She is confident and feels equal to anyone

Her death is tragic because it was avoidable

Minnie's death is as sudden as it is tragic. One day, she is killed at the factory where she works when she is pulled into the machinery by her long hair. The tragedy is that, if she had tied her hair back as she was supposed to, the accident would not have happened. Lily is terribly upset, and fantasizes about saving Minnie from the machine at the last moment, although she knows that, even if she had been there, there is nothing she could have done. Part of Lily's sadness is for Minnie's lost future, with a husband and children, which she will now never have. She has lost her life through "one tiny miscalculation, one moment of distraction" (pg. 97). In a way, Lily's cutting her hair after Minnie's funeral is her tribute to her friend: Lily wants to make sure she herself does not suffer a similar fate, and show that she has learnt from the tragedy.

Rooster

➟ Rooster becomes Lily's main ally in Red Lake and remains a good friend of the family.	Rooster

Lily first meets Rooster – whose real name is Orville Stubbs – the second time she is working as a teacher in Red Lake. She gives him his nickname because his thin legs look like a rooster's and, even after they become friends, the name sticks. He is a part-time deputy in the town and, at their first meeting, wants to have some fun at her expense by making her ride his wild mustang. He shows his prejudice against someone who was not born locally: "I hear you come all the way from Chicago to teach us hicks a thing or two" (pg. 120). He and his friend are so sure that Lily will be thrown from the horse that they cannot stop laughing, even before anything has happened. Lily, of course, wipes the smile off their faces by controlling and riding the horse: "I could tell it was killing them that I could get the best of a horse that must have given them plenty of trouble" (pg. 121). Following this incident, Rooster's attitude towards Lily changes from mockery to respect: he "started acting like my faithful sidekick, as if, since I'd bested him at a game of his own devising, he owed me his utter devotion" (pg. 122). Once she gets to know him, Lily finds he is "a likable little guy" (ibid.), even though he has some rather unrefined habits, such as swallowing his chewing tobacco.

The first time they meet, Rooster tries to make fun of Lily

Lily gains his respect and his friendship

Rooster works a lot with horses, and, through him, Lily gets to know the town's other horsemen. He encourages her to start horse racing again, and, after one of these races, he introduces her to Jim Smith, her future husband, although of course she does not know this at the time. In fact, initially Rooster is the one who is "sweet" on her (pg. 123), but she is quick to nip this in the bud by telling him that, after the failure of her first marriage, she did not want to get married again. They still remain friends, and in fact Rooster comes to trust Lily so much that he asks her to teach him to read and write, although he is clearly embarrassed by this request. Lily agrees, and gives him secret lessons on Saturday afternoons.

Rooster is the one who introduces her to Jim Smith

She teaches him to read and write

She trusts him to help her out

Rooster often helps Lily, sometimes in difficult situations. For example, after her sister commits suicide, Jim and Rooster are the two people she trusts to go with her and bury Helen in the countryside. When Lily and Jim get married, Rooster is Jim's best man. He is also the one who helps them move to the ranch near Seligman when their garage goes bankrupt. He always thinks that Jim is lucky to have married Lily, showing that he still has some feelings for her, although he accepts that she does not feel the same way about him: "You know I always been carrying a torch for you" (pg. 171). He asks Lily whether she thinks he'll ever get married, and she is suddenly sure that, somewhere, there is the right woman for him: "You just got to look in unexpected places" (ibid.). Sure enough, when Rooster is invited to Rosemary and Rex's wedding, he brings the Apache girl who is now his wife.

He has always been in love with Lily, but in the end finds the right woman for himself

Themes and Motifs

Ranch life versus city life

➟ At different times in her life, Lily chooses to live in a city. ➟ Although, each time, she enjoys city life at first, she discovers she is always happiest living in the heart of the countryside.	Ranch life versus city life

For a large part of her life, Lily lives on various ranches in New Mexico, Arizona and Texas. Having been born and spent most of her childhood on one, she is very familiar with the lifestyle and feels at home there. However, life is hard on these remote ranches, especially at the beginning of the 20th century when Lily is growing up: people lived with an almost complete lack of the modern appliances and conveniences that we take for granted today. On the other hand, anyone who lived on a ranch had the kind of freedom and independence that was not really possible in a city.

Lily was born and grew up on a ranch

Ranch life is hard but has a lot of freedom

Ranch life at the time tended to be rough, tough and very basic – there were certainly no luxuries, and no basic facilities, such as indoor bathrooms and toilets, either. However, most ranchers did not miss or even want indoor plumbing: "most people, including Mom and Dad, thought the idea of an indoor bathroom was vile and disgusting. 'Who in the Lord's name would want a crapper in the house?' Dad asked" (pg. 35). In fact, Lily does not get her first indoor toilet until she and Jim move to Ash Fork. Likewise, in the early part of the 20th century, electricity had not yet reached remote areas such as west Texas, resulting in even more hard physical work: "you had to do everything by hand, heating irons on the stove to press Mom's blouses, cooking cauldrons of lye and potash over the fire to make soap, working the pump, then toting clean water in to wash the dishes and dirty water out to pour on the vegetable garden" (ibid.).

A lack of basic comforts, although most people do not miss them

Ranch life involves hard physical work

Anyone living on a ranch was constantly at the mercy of the elements. The area around the family's homestead

Ranchers had to deal with hard conditions

on Salt Draw is part of the "rolling gritty grassland of west Texas" (pg. 17) and is a tough place to live. As Lily's father says, it "wasn't a place for the soft of head or the weak of heart" (ibid.). The countryside is flat, and everything – people, animals, even the water in the river – moves slowly in order to save energy. The ground is hard as rock most of the time, but is turned to mud from time to time when there is a flash flood. On all of the ranches on which she lives, Lily emphasizes the need for a good water supply: without it, there is no way of making a good living from the land and the animals raised there. Their ranch on Salt Draw runs along by the river, "so it was ten times more valuable than land without water" (ibid.), enabling them to train carriage horses and keep other animals, too. On the first ranch that Jim and Lily run, they persuade the English owners to pay to have dams built to store water from the occasional rains, thereby allowing them to raise far more cattle than would otherwise be possible.

A good water supply is essential

The importance of the weather forecast

It is essential for ranchers to know what the weather is going to be like, which is why she and Jim go to the considerable expense of buying a radio and generators to power it. They tune in every day to listen to the forecast so that they know what to expect and can plan accordingly:

> "With water so scarce and severe storms so dangerous – drowning or freezing cattle, flattening barns, washing away entire families, the lightning electrocuting horses with steel shoes – we lived and died by those forecasts" (pg. 186).

Severe droughts can ruin a rancher's livelihood

In the Arizona desert, serious droughts happen every ten years or so, and the rains, when they come, can be in the form of terrible, destructive storms. Ranchers who are unprepared for either of these possibilities can lose everything. This nearly happens to Lily and Jim once, when they have to live through more than a year without rain. Even the dams they have built dry out, and they have to buy water in order to survive. The first rains after the drought nearly burst the dams, but, thanks to Jim's skill and a good deal of luck, the ranch survives.

Despite the hardships of being a rancher, Lily and her family love ranch life – they love the freedom it gives them. On the one hand, they are free to run the place however they like, even though they do not own it: "I knew how lucky we were not just to have work but to be our own bosses doing something we were good at doing" (pg. 169). But it is more than this: the ranch itself means freedom for them. Lily, Jim and their children love living in the middle of the countryside, working in the open air and not having to worry about what others think. The children are able to run wild and are really at one with nature. Moreover, Lily feels an emotional attachment to the land that her father and grandfather owned and made a living from. It is more than just a place to live – for her, it means a direct connection with nature:

The freedom of being their own bosses

Emotional connection to the land

> "There was nothing to compare with standing on a piece of land you owned free and clear. [...] The soil belonged to you, and so did every rock, every blade of grass, every tree, and all the water and minerals under the land all the way to the center of the earth" (pg. 248).

This is why it is so important to her to keep the homestead on Salt Draw that her father leaves to her in his will – selling it would have been like selling a part of herself.

Lily does not want to sell the land she inherits

Lily does not spend all of her life on ranches. She also lives and works in various small towns and villages and, twice, in large cities, namely Chicago and Phoenix. In both cases, she moves to the city with high hopes and, although she likes living there at first, ends up disappointed. When she goes to live in Chicago, Lily is single and is looking for a place with opportunities for a young woman like herself: "I wanted to go where the opportunities were the greatest, where the future was unfolding right before your eyes. I wanted to go to the biggest, most boomingest city I could find" (pg. 91). At first, everything about the place is new and exciting, and a stark contrast to the remote ranches and towns in which she has lived up to now: the crowds, the noise, the buildings. One of the most fascinating aspects of the city is Lake Michigan:

She sees Chicago as a place of opportunity

At first she loves living in the city

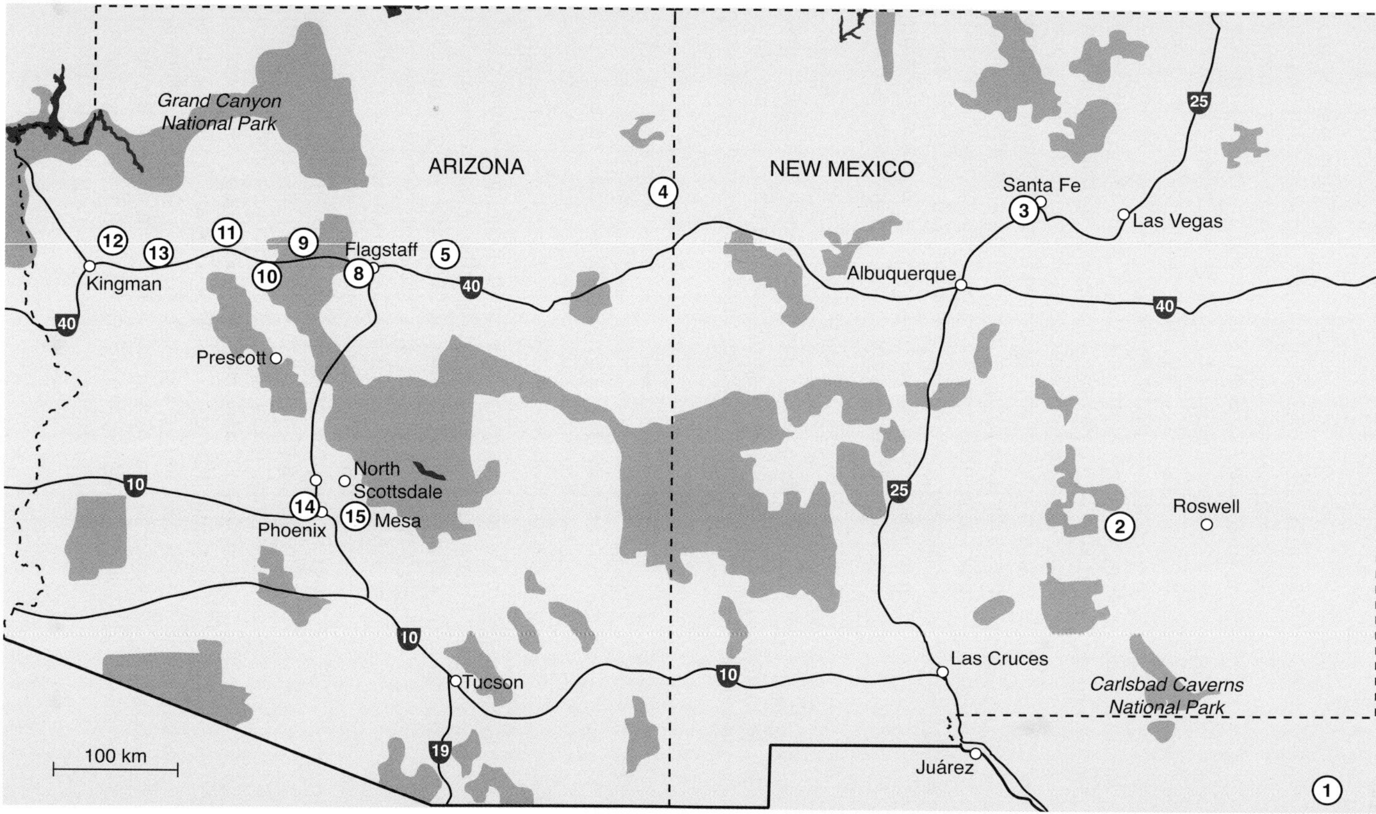
Grand Canyon
National Park
ARIZONA
NEW MEXICO
Santa Fe
Las Vegas
Kingman
Flagstaff
Albuquerque
Prescott
North
Scottsdale
Phoenix
Mesa
Roswell
Tucson
Las Cruces
Carlsbad Caverns
National Park
Juárez
100 km
40
10
25
19
1
2
3
4
5
8
9
10
11
12
13
14
15

Map of the places where Lily lived

1. Salt Draw (near Burnt Spring Hills, Texas) -> flows into the Pecos River, west Texas
   -> nearest town: Toyah, Texas -> four miles away
2. KC Ranch on the Rio Hondo, Hondo Valley, New Mexico -> south of the Capitan Mountains, 6 miles from Tinnie
3. Santa Fe -> school: The Sisters of Loretto Academy of Our Lady of the Light (the Miraculous Staircase is in the Loretto Chapel)
4. Red Lake, Coconino County, Arizona
5. Cow Springs – Leupp – Happy Jack – Greasewood – Wild Ruin
6. Back to the KC Ranch (see no. 2)
7. Chicago
8. Flagstaff
9. Red Lake (see no. 4)
10. Ash Fork
11. The ranch near Seligman, Arizona (the ranch is 15 miles west of Seligman along Route 66, then 9 miles off Route 66 along a dirt track)
12. Neighboring ranch, the Hackberry ranch, between the Peacock and the Walapai Mountains, Yavapai County
13. Main Street and Peach Strings, Arizona, where Lily works as a teacher
14. Phoenix (while she studies for her teaching degree) and where the whole family lives for a while
15. Horse Mesa (near the Horse Mesa Dam, Arizona)

> "Coming from a place where people measured water by the pailful, where they fought and sometimes killed each other over water, it was hard to imagine, even though I was looking at it, that billions of gallons of fresh water [...] could be sitting there undrunk, unused, and uncontested" (pg. 92).

The people are unfriendly

However, before long she discovers that the people are not as friendly as she is used to, and most of them seem to ignore each other: "I was used to nodding when I caught a stranger's eye, but here in Chicago they looked right through you, as if you weren't there at all" (pg. 93). Despite this, she loves living in the city, as it is "bold and bawdy and very modern" (pg. 95); in other words, a complete contrast to life on the ranch.

There are few job opportunities for someone without qualifications

Unfortunately, Lily soon finds out that there are not as many opportunities for someone like her as she expected. She has no real teaching qualifications so cannot get a job as a governess, as she had planned to do. Without any other skills or experience, the only jobs open to her are factory work or a position as a maid. Working as a maid does not suit her personality. Used to being everyone's equal and speaking her mind, she discovers that she is expected to keep her opinions to herself and behave humbly, as her employers clearly feel they are superior to her. Furthermore, Chicago is the place that Lily loses her only real friend, Minnie, and ends up marrying a bigamist who steals most of the money she has saved up. This leads her to conclude that it "was over between me and Chicago. The city, for all its beautiful blue water and soaring skyscrapers, had been nothing but heartache. It was time for me to get back to the range" (pg. 109). She feels regret at leaving: one of the reasons she came to the city was to live in a place full of the future-looking modern technology that was completely lacking back on the ranch: "I had come to Chicago wanting a slice of that modernity, loving the city for it, but Chicago hadn't loved me back" (pg. 111). Her main problem is that everything she did in Chicago was ultimately pointless, and she realizes that nobody there will even miss her when she is gone. In order to feel needed again, she has to go back to a place where she can do a job that counts for something.

Fate deals Lily many blows in Chicago

She regrets leaving, but sees no point in staying

After losing their job running the ranch in Arizona, Lily and Jim decide to make a clean break and try living in Phoenix, which was becoming a boom town. Lily is the only member of the family who really likes living there when they first move. She enjoys living somewhere that, for once, is not remote, and likes being able to walk to the shops, go to the movies, eat in restaurants and cafeterias. They buy a house with all the modern conveniences, such as indoor plumbing, get themselves new furniture, a new car, even a phone. They invest some of their savings in property and enjoy a comfortable lifestyle, especially compared with the rough living arrangements on the ranch. The children, however, hate the city from the outset with its concrete streets and strange noises. They feel "penned in" (pg. 273), missing the freedom of the countryside and being surrounded by nature: "'You can't even see the ground,' Rosemary complained. 'It's all covered up with pavement and sidewalks'" (ibid.). Jim, too, soon becomes dissatisfied because he is stuck in a rather boring desk job that does not make any use of his talents and experience as a rancher.

Lily likes the convenience of the city when they first move to Phoenix

The children hate the city

Before long, Lily begins to lose her affection for the city, too. For one thing, she is forced to drive carefully and pay attention to the rules of the road, whereas in the countryside "you drove wherever you wanted at whatever speed you wanted, and left the road whenever you were so inclined" (pg. 274). One reason Lily loves driving is for the sense of freedom it gives her, so it is not surprising that she feels caged in whenever she gets stuck in a traffic jam. As well as this, she starts to worry about all kinds of things that she never even had to consider on the ranch. In particular, she becomes nervous about crime, holding her bag tightly when she is out and keeping her revolver under the bed. After a while, she does not enjoy listening to the radio, because the news seems to consist of stories about robberies, burglaries, shootings and stabbings. Without realizing it, she has become a "worrywart" (pg. 276), and is not really able to relax, even at home. Generally, she mistrusts her fellow citizens; when this leads to her suspecting Jim of having an affair, the family decides it is probably time to leave the city and find a place to live where they can all feel at

Soon Lily also feels restricted by the city

She becomes nervous about things she never worried about before home again. They are the kind of people who need the freedom of wild, remote places rather than the constraints of city life.

Education and teaching

Education and teaching	
	➟ A good education is very important to Lily, and she works hard to get one. ➟ As a teacher, she is highly committed to her calling.

Lily and her siblings have little formal education

Throughout the story, it is clear that education and learning are very important to Lily. As children, neither she and her siblings, nor, later, Rosemary and Little Jim, have very much formal education. This is because, living as they do in remote places, the schools are either too far away, or, if they exist, only cover the first few grades.

They are taught by their father

Lily, Buster and Helen are taught by their father at first. Somewhat unusually, he himself had had a governess as a child and is well-read, making him well-equipped to tutor his own children on a wide range of subjects: "grammar, history, arithmetic, science, and civics" (pg. 31).

Dad teaches history with a biased slant

In particular, he teaches them a lot of history, although a rather biased version of events, with the English Pilgrims as the villains: "a bunch of pious hypocrites [...] who declared all men equal but kept slaves and massacred peaceful Indians" (ibid.), and the Irish as the heroes. Her father is convinced that his children are learning much more from him than they would at the local school. However, he feels it is important for them to get at least some formal education: "Because in this world, Dad said, it's not enough to have a fine education. You need a piece of paper to prove you got it" (pg. 32).

Of all the family, Lily is the most interested in learning

Of the three siblings, Lily is the only one who is really interested in learning. In the early part of the 20th century, however, it was not really considered necessary for girls to have a good education, an opinion that her parents share. Both she and Buster are sent away to school as teenagers, but Lily is the one who has to leave again when her father spends her tuition fees, even though she loves being at school and is doing very well there. Buster is not particularly academically minded, but since he is the boy, his parents believe it is more important for him to stay on at school, as he will have to run the ranch one day. Lily is struck by the unfairness of this, and is very angry with her father because of it, but there is nothing she can do about it.

Buster's education is seen as more important than Lily's

Nonetheless, Lily remains determined to get a good education and some qualifications, and never gives up on this goal. While living in Chicago, she goes to night school to get her high school diploma, which she achieves at the age of twenty-six. After this, she applies to do a teacher training course in Flagstaff, but does not even complete her first year there after being offered another teaching job in Red Lake. It is not until she is in her late thirties that she finally completes her college degree and gets her teaching diploma. She does this by working extremely hard, putting in eighteen-hour days and studying non-stop. Once again, it is clear that she loves learning, as she "felt happier than I thought I had a right to be" (pg. 237). She finally achieves her ambition of becoming a qualified teacher.

Lily never gives up until she finally gets her teaching diploma

Lily is, however, the only one in her family with a lot of enthusiasm for education. Her brother Buster is sent to school because he is a boy, but he is not really interested in learning much more than the basic skills he will need to run the ranch, while Helen never goes to school at all. Her own children are sent away to school a couple of times, and both even go to university, although her son drops out in his first year, but the formal atmosphere and rules of school do not suit children like them who are used to running wild on a ranch. Although Lily realizes they will find it difficult to settle down at first, she cannot really understand their attitude towards school, because it is so different from her own: "I had loved my time at the Sisters of Loretto when I was a girl, and I was sure that as soon as Rosemary got over her homesickness, she'd be fine" (ibid.). She thinks that her daughter should be grateful for the opportunity to go to school; in fact, Rosemary never gets over her homesickness and so never really gets the full benefit of school.

Her own children lack interest in education

Lily cannot understand why they do not love school like she did

Teaching at small schools allows Lily to make a difference

Most children in the remote parts of the south-west that Lily and her family live in do not get much more formal education than what they learn in small, one-room schools like those where Lily teaches. She finds the job extremely satisfying, because she can really make a difference to children's lives by teaching them the basic skills they need to get on in life: "It was good work, the kind of work that let you sleep soundly at night and, when you awoke, look forward to the day" (pg. 85). It seems that teaching is what she is called to do, and she is good at her job: "I never met a kid I couldn't teach" (ibid.). Moreover, she likes working in these small schools because she is her own boss and can teach what she likes and how she likes. Having to follow other people's instructions and deal with lots of paperwork, as is the case when she is working at the school in Phoenix, does not suit her personality; in fact, it is the only time she does not enjoy being a teacher.

She enjoys being her own boss

However, for Lily, teaching is not just confined to the classroom. Learning is very important to her, and she passes this on to her children from a young age. She starts trying to teach the three-year-old Rosemary her numbers and spellings: "If she asked for a glass of milk, I told her she could have it only if she spelled out 'milk'" (pg. 184). Lily cannot understand her daughter's lack of interest in these matters: "math and spelling confused here, and answering questions on cue bored her" (ibid.). She feels that her daughter will never get on well in life if she is unable to focus on the basics, and does not seem able to accept that Rosemary is just a young child who does not really need to know these things right now. Lily's determination to make her daughter learn, even though she is clearly not interested, is part of her ongoing attempt to change her daughter's character to make it more like her own. She often seems insensitive to her daughter's needs, giving more priority to teaching her a lesson than to providing emotional support. For example, when Rosemary is at school, she writes letters to her parents about how homesick she is and about her fears – the Second World War is still in progress and the news of Japanese bombers frightens her. Lily does not seem to know how to respond to this: "Be strong, was all

She wants her children to learn all kinds of lessons from a young age

Lily wants to change her daughter

I could think to say when I wrote back" (pg. 239). Although her daughter needs comfort more than anything else, Lily's main concern still seems to be her English skills: "I also corrected the grammar in her letters and returned them to her. I wouldn't have been doing that girl any favors to let those sorts of errors go unchecked" (ibid.). Teaching Rosemary often takes priority over simply being there for her when she needs her mother.

She seems insensitive to Rosemary's needs

And, of course, it is not only academic skills that Lily wants to pass on to her children. Equally as important to her are the lessons to be learned from life experience. Her attitude, based partly on her own experiences, of course, is that "the world was a dangerous place and life was unpredictable" (pgs. 183-184). This is why she feels it is essential to learn from the things that life throws at you, and from the mistakes you make. One of her often repeated phrases, certainly one that her daughter frequently has to hear, is "Let that be a lesson to you" (pg. 183). Moreover, she is not above using punishment to get her message across. One example is when Rosemary pretends to be feeling ill to get out of school. The classes have already been cancelled once that day, because Little Jim was injured and Lily thought he needed to go to hospital. However, after he makes a sudden recovery, Lily is determined not to waste the day and decides to collect all her students again so that they can go to school after all. Rosemary is not at all pleased by this turn of events, and thinks that if she pretends to be ill her mother will take her home again. Unfortunately for her, Lily sees through this ploy and, instead of taking her home, takes her to hospital: "I arranged for Rosemary to spend the night in a room by herself where she could ponder truth and consequences" (pg. 216). After a night alone, Rosemary is deemed to have learnt her lesson; certainly she never tries to get out of school again. Lily at least is satisfied with the outcome of her teaching methods.

Lily constantly tries to teach her children life lessons

She teaches through punishment

However, as the story progresses, it becomes clear that Rosemary does not learn the lessons that her mother expects her to learn. The constant pressure from her mother teaches Rosemary that she wants to be free to

Rosemary refuses to learn the lessons her mother wants to teach her choose how to live her own life, even if her mother does not approve. Lily does not seem to understand this, but continues to try to make her daughter follow her advice, right up to the time when Rosemary leaves home to get married. Lily's reaction to her daughter's insistence that she marries Rex is "Haven't I taught you anything?" (pg. 319), demonstrating that she is still unable to see things from Rosemary's point of view. It is Jim who, in the end, helps her to accept that she cannot change her daughter: Rosemary needs to be free. It is hard for Lily to admit that she has not managed, as she sees it, to teach her daughter what is important in life, but she finally understands that it is so: "So this is a lesson for me, then?" (pg. 320) she asks her husband. Jim shows her that Rosemary is happy and that she needs to let her go. We see in the end that Lily has learnt this lesson, but very reluctantly, and we can imagine her often saying 'I told you so' to her daughter in the years ahead.

Lily has to learn a lesson

Religion

Religion	➟ Lily does believe in God, but is not a deeply religious person and has some doubts about whether everything that happens is really God's will.

Her mother is very religious

Religion does not play a pivotal role in Lily's life, but it is a theme that recurs at different times during her story and influences her life in different ways.

Lily does not believe that her mother's prayers saved them from the flash flood

Right at the start of the story, we discover that Lily's mother is deeply religious. When her three children return home after a night spent in a tree to avoid being swept away from the flash flood, her first reaction upon seeing them is to fall on her knees in prayer. In fact, she takes credit for their safe return: "It was she who had saved us, she declared, by staying up all night praying" (pg. 16). She says her children need to thank her and their guardian angel that they are still alive. Buster and Helen are influenced by their mother's beliefs and obediently join her in prayer. Lily is more skeptical about her mother's role in their survival: "The way I saw it, I was the one who'd saved us all, not Mom and not some guardian angel. No one was up in that cottonwood tree except the three of us" (ibid.). It is typical of Lily's practical nature that she believes in hard facts rather than in an invisible power that supposedly helped them. In this instance, her father comforts her by telling her that she herself might have been the guardian angel.

Lily is annoyed when her mother prays rather than helping

At other times, her mother's insistence on praying rather than helping makes her angry. During another big flood which strikes while her father is away on business, her mother once again retreats to high ground with Buster and Helen to pray, leaving the eight-year-old Lily and the two servants, Apache and Lupe, to try and save the dugout. It is a desperate situation, yet when Mom returns to the dugout, it is not to help, but to try and get Lily, Apache and Lupe to join her in prayer. Lily responds angrily: "'To heck with praying!' I shouted. 'Bail, dammit, bail!'" (pg. 27). Her mother is shocked by this reaction: "I could tell she thought I'd probably doomed us all with my blasphemy" (ibid.), and Lily admits that she herself is slightly shocked by what she has just said. However, she knows that they will never save their home by praying, but they might have a chance if everyone helps. Unfortunately, her mother chooses to continue praying, and the dugout collapses under the masses of water. Mom's justification for not helping is that the flood is the will of God, and that they should submit to this, accepting their fate. Lily disagrees: "Submitting seemed to me a lot like giving up. If God gave us the strength to bail […] isn't that what he wanted us to do?" (pg. 28). This viewpoint is tested after the flood, when the family is able to salvage wood from an abandoned ranch and build themselves a proper house. For Mom, this is confirmation that the flood was God's will, because they are now far better off because of it. The incident leaves Lily feeling uncertain what to believe: "Mom could say that in hindsight, but it seemed to me that when you were in the middle of something, it was awful hard to figure out what part of it was God's will and what wasn't" (ibid.). Her father's opinion on the matter makes things a little clearer for her, and influences her throughout her life: "God deals us all different

Mom thinks they have to submit to the will of God

Lily is not sure what can be considered God's will

hands. How we play 'em is up to us" (pg. 29). In other words, rather than blindly accepting everything that happens as God's will, it is important to make the most of the situations we are faced with.

She does not rely on prayer to help her

On the whole, Lily is not the kind of person who feels the need to rely on God and prayer. For example, when she has to leave the convent school because there is no money left for her fees, it would be possible for her to stay if she decided to become a nun. She briefly considers the idea, feeling she owes God something for having saved her family during the tornado that ultimately forced them to leave Salt Draw. However, she already knows in her heart that "I wasn't cut out to be a nun. [...] I was just too restless a soul. And I didn't like taking orders from anyone, not even the pope" (pg. 59). As the story progresses, her contacts with the church and religion are often unpleasant experiences. For example, the residents of Red Lake do not find out about her sister's pregnancy until Helen faints one day at church and the Catholic priest condemns her as a sinner. The shame she is made to feel is certainly a contributing factor in her suicide. In addition to this, the priest refuses Helen a Catholic burial, so Lily has to find somewhere else as her final resting place. With Jim and Rooster's help, she buries her sister on a hillside in the heart of the country, a place "so beautiful that I knew in God's eyes it must be sacred" (pg. 141). Here, Lily seems defiant of organized religion while believing in God's presence in the natural world.

Lily knows she would not make a good nun

She defies organized religion

From time to time, Lily has to deal with followers of other religions, but these encounters are usually unsatisfactory. When she is heavily pregnant with her first child, she is visited by a Jehovah's Witness, a religion she is normally sympathetic towards, and becomes increasingly irritated by his insistence that she should convert for the sake of her child. She is furious at his presumption that he knows what is right for her: "Who the hell was he to tell me what I had to believe? I asked. All folks needed to find their own way to heaven" (pg. 150). This reflects her general attitude that people need to be able to think for themselves, and decide for them-

She doesn't like being told what to believe

selves what they want to believe. Later, when teaching in a remote town where most of her students come from a very strict Mormon community, she tries to get this message across to the girls in her school. Seeing that these girls are basically being raised to be wives and produce as many children as possible, Lily feels a strong need to let them know there is another world outside their religious community, one with a variety of opportunities and ways of living. Although she respects their right to believe what they like, she realizes that they have not been told that there is any other way to live, and she sees it as her duty "to make sure the girls I was teaching learned that it was a big world out there and there were other things they could do besides being broodmares dressed in feed sacks" (pg. 209). Her students are very interested in her stories about the wider world, but the local elders are very angry that she is, as they see it, trying to lead the children astray by telling them that "people were free to think for themselves and follow their hearts when it came to matters of faith" (pg. 212). One of these elders threatens Lily, to the extent that she pulls her gun on him, even firing a shot in warning. Unsurprisingly, she loses her job: the people in the town do not want to change their beliefs and make sure she is removed before she can put too many ideas into their children's heads.

She wants to tell the Mormon girls about alternatives to the life they are supposed to lead

Lily loses her job when she tries to get the girls to think for themselves

Horses

Horses	➟ Lily learns to break horses as a young child and they remain important to her. ➟ She often uses the metaphor of people being like "half-broke horses".

She has worked with horses from a young age

All her life, Lily has worked with horses. As a young girl, she learns how to train them from her father and, according to him, has "horse blood in her veins" (pg. 75). In fact, he cannot understand why she wants to become a teacher when she could continue working with horses: "training horses was more fun than drilling illiterate kids their ABCs, why would I want to be cooped up in a classroom when I could be out on the range?" (pg. 73). Horses are always part of her life, but she feels called to do more than simply be a horse-trainer. In fact, when she returns to the ranch after her first stint as a teacher, she knows this is not what she wants to do any more. Dad is puzzled by her reluctance to go out to the corral with him to work with some new horses he has got, but, having had a taste of the wider world, Lily knows "it was not the life I wanted" (pg. 90).

She does not want to work as a horse-trainer all her life

The importance of understanding horses in order to train them

Although Dad's disabilities were caused by a horse, he loves horses "because, unlike people, they always understood him and never pitied him" (pg. 19). He knows that the horse that kicked him was only acting on instinct, and does not blame it for his injuries. He teaches Lily that, in order to train them, you have to be able to "think like a horse" (pg. 36), and teach the animal that you will protect him. Dad's training methods do not involve beating the horses, but instead he uses gentler means so that the horses are not frightened of him. Lily's job is to break the horses, i.e. get them used to having a rider. This is quite an easy job with her father's carriage horses, as they have lived with people all their lives. However, from time to time, she still gets thrown, once breaking her arm badly. For Dad, this is a valuable lesson: "Most important thing in life [...] is learning how to fall" (pg. 38). He also teaches her that it is important to get up and try again after a fall, something that she

People who work with horses need to know how to fall and get up again puts into practice at different times in her life when faced with problems.

Half-broke horses are only partly tame

From time to time, Lily also has to deal with half-broke horses. These are wild mustangs sometimes used by cowboys when rounding up cattle out on the range. The cowboys capture them, ride them for a couple of days and then, more often than not, simply let them go again. For the cowboys, staying on these wild horses is a matter of pride, and they do not take the time to train them properly. As a result, the horses are afraid of people but, through human contact, lose some of the instincts they need to survive in the wild. On the other hand, they tend to be intelligent animals that make good horses if properly broken and trained. Lily herself has a mare, Patches, that starts out as a half-broke horse. Patches is her faithful companion when she makes the long journey to Red Lake, and stays with her throughout her time as an itinerant teacher. Lily has to leave Patches behind at the KC Ranch when she moves to Chicago, but collects her again when she returns to Red Lake for the second time. From then onwards, Patches stays with Lily as a working horse until the family moves to Phoenix, at which point Lily gives her to the local Havasupai tribe, allowing her to spend the rest of her life in beautiful surroundings.

Lily's horse Patches starts off as a half-broke horse

She enjoys horse-racing

As well as working with horses, Lily enjoys racing them, first Patches and, later, Rooster's horse Red Devil. Because she often wins, the races are an additional source of income for her, as well as getting her a reputation as the "horse-race-winning schoolmarm of Coconino County" (pg. 123), a reputation she feels very comfortable with. It is also through horse-racing that she meets Jim Smith, her second husband, a love of horses being one of the things that connects them.

She and Jim share a love of horses

The young cowboys on the ranch are half-broke horses

Lily also uses the phrase "half-broke horses" to describe people who do not seem completely tame. One such group is the young cowboys who work on Lily and Jim's first ranch. Most of them are Mexican or Native American from the Havasupai tribe, and are "misfits, […] runaways and boys who'd been whipped too hard" (pg. 177).

They are proud of their ability to stay on a horse and are extremely tough, and are well-suited to their hard job. Unsurprisingly, they have not learned how to live in civilized society, and in the bunkhouse in which they sleep there is "nonstop cussing, drinking, brawling, card play, and knife play" (pg. 178). Rosemary has to keep away from the bunkhouse as Lily does not trust the cowboys around a young, pretty girl like her. Part of the trouble is that Rosemary herself is a half-broke horse. As a child, she runs wild on the ranch, is tough and wants all animals to live free, whether domestic animals or wild ones. When she goes away to school, her wild nature becomes even more noticeable when contrasted with the genteel behavior of her fellow pupils. She finds it impossible to adapt to the more civilized lifestyle that is expected of her there; as a result, she remains an outsider and never manages to settle down at school. Likewise, as an adult, she is happiest living in remote places, free of rules and other constraints. It is not surprising that she chooses to marry Rex, someone who, like her, does not like to live by the rules, and prefers wild adventures to a conventional lifestyle. Lily does what she can to make Rosemary change her mind, believing a sensible, steady man would be far better for her wild daughter, but in the end she has to accept Rosemary's choice. The couple leave their wedding reception "heading out into open country like a couple of half-broke horses" (pg. 322) – this is a clear indication that their married life will continue to be wild and unconventional, as indeed turns out to be the case.

Rosemary is as untamed as a half-broke horse, and has problems adapting to civilized society

Rex is another untamed creature, just like Rosemary

Cars and planes

Cars and planes	➟ Lily is fascinated by technology, and loves the freedom cars and planes give her.

Lily is enthusiastic about modern transport

Although she loves horses, Lily is unsentimental about the inevitability of technological progress, and is very enthusiastic about the possibilities that modern forms of transport, such as cars and planes, can bring. She knows that the days of transport by horse and carriage are numbered: "I'd seen a number of automobiles in my years in Arizona, and they gave me a sinking feeling about the future prospects for carriages – and carriage horses" (pg. 90). This 'sinking feeling' is mainly due to concern about her father, as she knows that he prefers to live in the past and does not accept that cars are the future: "No one'll ever look as smart in one of those fume belchers as they do in a carriage" (ibid.). This is an attitude that Lily finds irritating, because she knows that progress cannot be stopped. This is one reason she decides to leave the ranch for good – she wants to be part of the wider world, a place of cars and planes and opportunities.

Unlike her father, she accepts that cars are inevitable

Cars represent opportunity

Cars play a role in Lily's relationship with Jim Smith. They first meet at a horse race he is judging, during which Lily is thrown from her horse after a car backfires. She learns that Jim owns the local garage. He presumes that she is not keen on cars; however, she tells him that she would love to learn to drive. Jim offers to teach her, which is the start of their friendship. Driving quickly becomes one of Lily's passions: "I discovered that I loved cars even more than I loved horses" (pg. 126). Practical as ever, she likes the fact that "[c]ars didn't need to be fed if they weren't working, and they didn't leave big piles of manure all over the place" (ibid.). Cars do want their owner wants them to do, which is perfect for someone like Lily who likes to be in control.

Jim and Lily first become friends when he teaches her to drive

Cars have several advantages over horses

At the start of their married life, Lily and Jim earn their living through cars, as Jim still has his garage. In the economic downturn, they are forced to sell the business; however, wherever they work from then on, they always have at least one car or pickup – a sure sign of the changing times that even ranchers no longer rely only on horses. Later, as part of one of her teaching jobs, she buys an old hearse that she uses as a school bus, driving around the countryside before and after school to collect her students, and then take them home again at the end of the day. Before long, it occurs to her that she can also use the hearse to run a taxi service at the weekends. Being able to drive means being able to make extra money, which she saves in the hope that she and Jim

Driving means freedom, and is also a way of making money

will be able to buy their own ranch one day. Above all, she loves the freedom that driving brings her. The only time she does not enjoy it so much is when she is driving in a city, as she then has to obey the traffic rules and cannot drive as fast as she likes. This is, of course, typical of her character: she dislikes having to follow any rules.

Lily's dislike of rules and regulations

Lily's other love is flying. She sees her first plane on the journey back from Red Lake to the KC Ranch and is tremendously excited by the sight of it. For one thing, seeing the plane in real life allows her to understand the science behind it. Moreover, for her the plane symbolizes an escape to a wider world, one full of new possibilities: "Another thing that airplane made me realize was that there was a whole world out there beyond ranchland that I'd never seen" (pg. 90). She can hardly wait to get out there, even learn to fly herself. It is quite a long time before she is able to achieve this ambition, but her chance comes one day when she and the family are out for a drive and see a sign for flying lessons in a field. The pilot's patronizing attitude to the idea of teaching a woman to fly shows how unusual this was for the time, but Lily shows him she is not afraid. She loves the feeling of flying, of being able to look down on the world from a distance: "Nothing had ever made me feel as free as flying" (pg. 274). Unfortunately, she is not able to complete her pilot's license in Phoenix, as she intended, because the flying school there is bound by what she sees as a lot of ridiculous rules. In order to continue her lessons, she would need an eye test and much more besides; of course, for Lily, these rules are just another way of restricting her freedom, rather than necessary safety measures. As a result, Lily does not get her pilot's license, but her love of flying remains, which is why she allows Rex to take her up in his plane. During their flight together, Rex does some daredevil maneuvers with the plane that would have terrified many people, but not Lily. Reluctant as she is to find anything good about her future son-in-law, flying is one of the things they have in common.

Like cars, planes symbolize the opportunities of the wider world

It is unusual for women to learn to fly

Lily and Rex share a love of flying

Playing the cards you've been dealt

→ This metaphor is used to show the importance of taking one's fate into one's own hands and making the best of any given situation.

Playing the cards you've been dealt

One of the book's recurring motifs is the idea of playing the cards you are dealt in life, of being master of your own fate instead of simply accepting it. This is certainly what Lily's father believes: the things that happen may be God's will, but people have a free choice when it comes to deciding how to deal with them. This view contrasts with that of his wife: for Mom, the only option is to submit to one's fate, and that it is almost blasphemous to try and change it. Dad's attitude here is an interesting one, as many would say that, with his disabilities and speech impediment, he had not been dealt a very good hand in life. However, he had managed to survive being kicked in the head as a young child and had gone on to run his own ranch, raise a family and pursue several interests, living a long, fulfilled life. He had lived by his own principles, which this is why Lily does not see his death as tragic: "He hadn't drawn the best of cards, but he'd played his hand darned well, so what was there to grieve over?" (pg. 246).

Dad strongly believes people are free to control their own fate

Dad appears to be someone who has been dealt a bad hand

Likewise, Lily believes in the importance of taking the opportunities that come her way. When she is offered her first teaching job, she knows she must take it. Her father, although he is not keen on the idea of her leaving the ranch, has to admit that this is the right thing for her to do: "Seems you been dealt a card, [...]. I guess you better go on and play it" (pg. 74). Throughout her story, she makes a good job of playing the cards she has been dealt, even if not all of the hands are good. When she discovers that her first husband is a bigamist, she has the marriage annulled so that she can start with a clean slate. Her sister Helen's suicide is a terrible blow to her, but something positive does come out of it, as it leads to her decision to ask Jim Smith to marry her. When Jim's and her garage is under threat of bankruptcy, she decides to sell bootleg liquor to keep them afloat

Lily often makes the best of bad situations

financially, but accepts that she has to stop when it becomes too dangerous. When Jim is fired as ranch manager and the family is forced to move away, she does not allow herself any regrets, but leaves without looking back.

She does not allow herself to regret the past

Lily is unhappy about Rosemary's choice of husband, and finds it very hard to accept that her daughter has gone against her wishes by marrying someone that she disapproves of. In the end, she is resigned to the marriage, although she realizes that their life together will be anything but ordinary. This is why Lily is determined to play an active part in her grandchildren's lives: she feels there is a lot she will need to teach them. However, she is sure the children will be survivors: "they came from hardy stock, and I figured they'd be able to play the cards they'd been dealt" (pg. 326). If they have inherited any of their grandmother's character, they will be able to handle any challenges they have to face.

Her grandchildren will probably not have an easy life, but Lily is sure they will be able to handle it

About the author

Jeannette Walls is Lily Casey Smith's second surviving grandchild, born on 21 April 1960. She is a writer and journalist who worked as a gossip columnist for msnbc.com, now NBCNews.com. She has also written for *New York Magazine* and *Esquire*, among other publications, but gave up journalism in 2007 to become a full-time writer.

"Half Broke Horses" is her second novel; her first, "The Glass Castle", is a best-selling memoir of her family, with particular emphasis on her unconventional childhood as the daughter of Rex and Rose Mary Walls. Their family is as dysfunctional as might be expected with these parents, and the children, Jeannette in particular, show a great deal of resilience in overcoming the disadvantages of their family life, while still remaining close.

For anyone who has read "Half Broke Horses", "The Glass Castle" makes an interesting follow-up read, as it continues the story of Lily's daughter and shows the effect her way of life had on her children. Jeannette Walls's third novel is fictional, called "The Silver Star" and was published in 2013.

Although "Half Broke Horses" is biographical, Jeannette Walls refers to it as a novel because she has had to use her imagination to fill in some of the details that were vague or could no longer be verified: she admits that it was never her aim to be completely historically accurate.

On the other hand, it is clear that calling the book a novel is not quite satisfactory to her. As she puts it: "I saw the book more in the vein of an oral history, a retelling of stories handed down by my family through the years, and undertaken with the storyteller's traditional liberties" (pg. 328). It is a mark of her talent as a storyteller that she is able to bring her grandmother to life so vividly and to "capture Lily's distinctive voice" (ibid.), which she achieves by writing in the first person. A lot of the stories in the book have come from her mother, whose detailed memories of her parents and various other facts about her childhood, such as the history and landscape of the places where they lived, formed the basis of the book.

Bibliography

Walls, Jeannette, *Half Broke Horses*, Ernst Klett Sprachen, Stuttgart, 2013.
– *The Glass Castle*, Schribner, New York, 2005.

Useful links: interviews with Jeannette Walls and reviews of her books
- https://www.youtube.com/watch?v=SFACYFtIGxI – Jeannette Walls talking about how she came to write "Half Broke Horses"
- http://en.wikipedia.org/wiki/Jeannette_Walls
- http://en.wikipedia.org/wiki/Half_Broke_Horses
- http://gothamist.com/2005/05/27/jeannette_walls_author_the_glass_castle_gossip_columnist_msnbccom.php
- http://leahpeah.com/interviews/jeannette-walls
- http://authors.simonandschuster.com/Jeannette-Walls/19723841

1. "Let that be a lesson to you."

1. What kinds of lessons does Lily try to teach her children and why?

2. How successful is she at getting her message across?

1.

Lily believes passionately in the importance of learning, and not just in a classroom context. As well as teaching her children to read and write, she wants to make sure they learn from life. She herself has had to cope with difficult situations from an early age. Even as a child, she has to take on a lot of responsibility on the family ranch, effectively running it at times, as her father is often away and her mother is too delicate to be of any practical help. As a teenager, she leaves home to become a teacher, living alone in small, remote towns for four years, before moving to Chicago, again alone, and making her way there. At all the different stages of her life, Lily has learnt from her experiences, some positive, some negative, and is left with the conviction that life has a lot to teach us and at times we have to learn the hard way. This is the message that she then tries to get across to her own children, particularly to her daughter.

From a young age, Rosemary shows that she does not see things the same way as her mother does: there is "a fundamental difference of opinion between her and me" (pg. 183), as Lily puts it. Lily is always certain that she is right in any given situation, and therefore sees it as her duty to point out to Rosemary what she has done wrong, or to show her how things could have been different. One example is Bossie the cow. The family has been given the gift of a pedigree Guernsey cow, one that gives very rich milk with good cream, and whose calves would be worth a lot of money when sold. Rosemary, however, hates the idea of any animal being fenced in, even domestic animals that are being protected for their own good. One day, somebody lets Bossie out of her stall. She goes into the granary and eats a huge amount of feed, too much for her to digest. By the time she is discovered, it is too late to save her, and she dies in terrible pain. Rosemary is distraught by her death, and Lily is extremely angry. The lesson in this case is clear: "Just you remember [...] that this is what could happen when an animal gets freedom. Animals act like they hate to be penned up, but the fact is, they don't know what to do with freedom. And a lot of times it kills them" (pg. 180). However, this incident does not seem to have changed Rosemary's attitude in the long run. When she is older, helping to round up the cattle so that they can be driven to market, she sometimes lets some of the cows escape. Lily tells her in no uncertain terms that this behavior is not consistent with her desire to live on a ranch all her life. The point of ranching is to raise cattle to sell for food: "If that upsets you – if you're rooting for the cattle to break free – you're not cut out for ranch life" (pg. 252). To prove her wrong, Rosemary decides to try the most unpleasant job on the ranch, skinning a steer. Although it makes her cry, she sees the job through to the end, but this time clearly has learnt something: that she is not cut out to be a rancher. In this case, Lily is proved right.

2.

Some of the time, Lily does manage to get her message through to her daughter, although perhaps not in the way that she originally intended. When the two of them are driving back to the KC Ranch with Lily's father's dead body in the back of the car, Rosemary becomes very embarrassed when passersby notice this and make remarks. However, Lily's attitude is that "Life's too short [...] to worry what other people think of you" (pg. 245). It can be said that Rosemary takes this lesson to heart later in her life. Certainly she rejects any attempts to encourage her to lead a conventional lifestyle, and in Rex Walls she finds a husband who does not care what people think of him, either. This, of course, was not Lily's intention at all. She wants her daughter to have a steady career as a teacher and to marry a sensible, solid man who will be an "anchor" (pg. 301) for her. She comes to realize, however, that Rosemary has never really listened to her opinion and probably never will. Rosemary confirms this on the night she tells her mother that she is going to marry Rex.

Still disapproving, Lily says: "Haven't I taught you anything?" (pg. 319). Her daughter's reply is significant: "You sure have. [...] That's all you've been doing my whole life. 'Let this be a lesson. Let that be a lesson.' But all these years, what you thought you were teaching me was one thing, and what I was learning was something else" (ibid.). It seems that the main lesson Rosemary has learnt from her mother is that she does not want to be like her. Lily feels that she has completely failed in her mission to teach her daughter about life. It is hard for her to accept that Rosemary has the right to live her life however she likes.

2. "Most important thing in life is learning how to fall."

1. How would you interpret this phrase in the context of Lily's life as a whole?

2. How does she deal with the times in her life when she 'falls'?

1.

When she is a young child, Lily's father teaches her about the importance of knowing how to fall. One of his sources of income is training and selling carriage horses, and Lily helps him to break the horses. Of course, they often throw her off their backs in the early stages of their training. Her mother is very worried that she will have a serious accident, and in fact she does once break her arm very badly. Her father, however, is not concerned about these accidents, maintaining that, as falling is inevitable, it is only a question of knowing how to do it properly. "Your body knows how to fall" (pg. 40) he tells her and, if she falls the right way, she will not hurt herself. In addition to this, he shows her that she should not be defeated by a fall, but should always try again. The next time, he says, she will do better.

2.

Perhaps as a result of her father's philosophy, Lily is not a person to be defeated by setbacks, although she suffers several in her life. One of the first of these that she experiences is when she goes away to boarding school at the age of thirteen. As someone who has always loved learning, Lily is very happy at school and takes full advantage of the opportunities to get an education. In addition to this, school life is so much easier than being on the ranch: she does not have any hard physical work to do, but can instead concentrate on studying. It is therefore a terrible blow to her when Mother Albertina, the school principal, informs her that her father no longer has any money to pay for her tuition fees and she will have to leave. As she leaves, Mother Albertina gives her a piece of advice that will also help her to deal with setbacks later in life: "When God closes a window, he opens a door. But it's up to you to find it" (pg. 60). Not long afterwards, Lily takes this advice to heart when Mother Albertina writes to suggest that she takes a test that will allow her to become a teacher, even without a diploma. She passes the test and is able to get her first teaching job, confirming for her that this is the job she really wants to do.

Another major setback Lily suffers is when she discovers that her first husband, Ted, already has a wife and children, and their whole relationship has been a lie. What is more, he has taken nearly all of their savings, most of which came from money Lily earned, and which was intended to fund her college education, enabling her to get her teaching diploma. Her first reaction when she finds out is shock, quickly followed by anger. She confronts Ted and he admits everything, but still tries to persuade her that he loves her and only lied so that he could be with her. This does not cut any ice with Lily: "The louse was acting as if he expected me to feel sorry for him" (pg. 108) and she tells him in no uncertain terms that it is over between them. She shows him that she now sees what kind of person he really is and that he has not crushed her spirit: "The fact is, you don't love me, and you haven't destroyed me. You don't have what it takes to do that" (ibid.). Although she is obviously very shaken by what has happened, she is determined to put her marriage behind her and make a clean break. Therefore she applies to have the marriage annulled, and throws her diamond engagement ring, which also turns out to be fake, into Lake Michigan. She decides to focus on getting a degree and becoming a teacher, and is sure she will never marry again after this experience; of course, she turns out to be wrong about this.

Lily is a very resourceful person, able to come up with a creative solution when faced with difficulties. One example of this is when her husband Jim's garage is threatened with bankruptcy due to the recession: many people have to sell their cars and tractors because they can no longer afford gas to run them. In addition to this, Jim often helps people out by repairing their cars for free or only charging them a small amount of money. Lily is sure there must be a way of making some additional cash and, when a friend of Jim's who sells bootleg liquor asks to hide it at their house, she hits upon the idea of becoming a seller, too. This goes well until she refuses to sell alcohol to a man who is obviously already drunk, and, in revenge, he reports her to the police. A couple of officers come round to her house, but believe her story that she is not the kind of person who would sell illegal drink. After that, she and Jim decide it would be best to end her career as a 'liquor lady'. However, she has managed to keep them afloat for a while, and, although they do in fact lose their garage a few months later, when this happens they are lucky enough to be offered the chance to run a ranch instead.

From time to time, Lily takes on teaching jobs to supplement their income on the ranch. She often ends up losing these jobs again, mainly because of her refusal to compromise her principles. In one such case, she is fired because she gives the town's deputy's son a beating for putting his hand up a girl's skirt. Unsurprisingly, the boy's father makes sure she loses her job. Lily is convinced that beating the boy was the right thing to do, that he has to be taught to treat girls with respect before it is too late. However, even she is surprised how strongly being fired affects her this time. When Rosemary comes into the room, she finds her mother crying with the letter of dismissal in her hand. Until that moment, Lily had not even noticed her own tears: "[…] by letting my own daughter see me all weak and pitiful, I felt that I'd failed her in a big way, and I was furious with myself" (pg. 227). She does not want Rosemary to see her as vulnerable in any way, but as someone who can overcome setbacks like this: "[…] I'm not weak. You'll never have to worry about that. Your mother is not a weak woman" (ibid.). Instead of crying at the kitchen table, she goes outside and relieves her frustration and anger by chopping wood with all her strength. She is also determined to find a way of showing the deputy and everyone else in the town that her spirit has not been broken. The opportunity to do so arises when a film premiere of *Gone with the Wind* is to be shown in a nearby town. Lily decides to attend the premiere, a gala event for which the audience is expected to dress up. She makes herself a striking evening dress and has Jim drive her right up to the red carpet in front of the movie theater. She makes a dramatic entrance in front of Deputy Johnson and is photographed as if she herself was a movie star. It is the perfect revenge.

Lily and her family love their new life on the ranch, but suffer a further setback some years later when the owners decide to sell it. There is nothing they can do about it, and, although they have some savings, it is not enough to buy a ranch of their own. Jim is very upset, because the main reason he loses his job is that the new owner considers him too old to keep on, despite all his years of experience. Although she is also upset, feeling as if they are losing all they have worked for in the course of the years, Lily is determined not to dwell on the past: "We've never felt sorry for ourselves before […] and we're not going to start now. Let's get packing" (pg. 266). They decide to try city life for a while and move to Phoenix. Before they go, they sell nearly all of their ranching equipment, including their horses, and as they are driving away she tells her son "No looking back. […] You can't. You just can't" (pg. 267). Her method of dealing with this particular setback is similar to how she dealt with the breakup of her first marriage: she cuts her losses and moves forward without thinking too much about what she has lost.

3. Lily's relationships with women

1. Lily lives and works very much in a man's world, and, as a result, generally gets on well with men. But how does she relate to the women in her life? Describe and analyze some of Lily's relationships with women.

As a child, Lily gets on much better with her father than with her mother. The two of them are similar in character: "we were both tough nuts" (pg. 17) and were therefore well-suited to life to the hard life in the wild, remote area in which they live. It "wasn't a place for the soft of head or the weak of heart" (ibid.) as her father puts it. Her mother, on the other hand, is a completely different kind of person: genteel, delicate and not cut out for the rough, tough ranch lifestyle. This does not always make the relationship between Lily and her mother easy. In fact, as she puts it: "Mom didn't quite know what to make of me" (pg. 34). Lily is not interested in being genteel, but is always outside, helping with the hard physical work on the ranch. Because she "didn't have the makings of a lady" (ibid.), her mother is worried that it will be difficult for her to find a good husband. Mom certainly admires Lily's courage and her ability to get things done – in fact, she relies heavily on her daughter, especially when her husband is away on one of his frequent trips – but she is not sure that her daughter's bravery is necessarily a good thing. Lily and her mother really are opposites: "Mom wasn't exactly the most useful person in the world" (ibid.). This is particularly frustrating for Lily at times when her mother's "help" consists of praying rather than doing something practical.

For example, when their dugout is in danger of collapsing during a severe storm, everybody is needed to help bail out the water. Mom, however, chooses instead to take her youngest two children to high ground to pray. Lily is furious: if her mother had helped, they might have managed to save their home. As it is, the dugout is destroyed. On the whole, though, Lily seems sympathetic towards her mother: she understands that, most of the time, Mom is trying to make the best of a life that she is not really suited to. She also sees that Mom does her best for her children by her own standards: brushing her daughters' hair until it shines and teaching them to be ladylike so that they will get good husbands. This is what most mothers at the time wanted for their daughters.

Lily has always taken care of her younger sister Helen: in the very opening scene, we see her saving Helen and her brother Buster from a flood. Like her mother, Helen is too delicate for the rough life on the ranch, and does not enjoy physical work that goes beyond baking and sewing. Lily thinks her sister is rather naive – her ambition is to move to Los Angeles and become a movie actress, but Lily wonders how she will manage there as she is "not the most self-reliant creature in the world" (pg. 115). After Helen moves to Hollywood, she and Lily remain close by regularly exchanging letters. Helen's letters are full of stories about auditions and film stars, about how she is sure it will not be long before she gets a part in a film. She also has a series of boyfriends: every time a new one comes along, she is convinced he will be the one to give her her big break in the movie world. It is clear to Lily that these men are taking advantage of her sister, and she does her best to warn Helen about the life she is leading. However, Helen does not listen to her sister's advice, and, sure enough, becomes accidently pregnant by one of her boyfriends, who then wants nothing more to do with her.

Lily is the one she turns to in this crisis, afraid that her parents will disown her. She is thinking about getting an abortion; Lily does not want her to do so, as women often died as a result, and instead invites Helen to come and stay with her while they work out what to do. When she arrives, Lily is immediately struck by how fragile and vulnerable her sister seems, and is determined to help her. However, Helen does not respond to any of Lily's suggestions: writing to their parents asking them to take her in, giving up the baby for adoption, marrying a man who'd be willing to take on the baby as well. All Helen can think about is how the pregnancy might damage her career. At first, Lily does not try to force her into a decision, but Helen's inability to be realistic soon starts to irritate her. This is when the difference in their personalities becomes clear: Lily is full of practical solutions, whereas Helen does not seem able to face up to reality. She has convinced herself that she will never be strong like Lily: "I just feel like giving up" (pg. 138). For Lily, this would never be an option, and she tries to encourage her sister with stories about how she overcame problems: "You're much stronger than you think. There's always a way out" (ibid.).

Despite her irritation at Helen's attitude, Lily is extremely protective of her, and behaves very tenderly towards her, holding her in her arms as she sleeps and taking her on outings in an attempt to cheer her up. What Lily does not predict is that Helen's 'way out' of the situation will be to hang herself. When this happens, there is further evidence of the sisters' close relationship: Lily, who has gone out to borrow a car, suddenly feels "like something was choking me" (pg. 139) and is "overtaken with a horrible feeling of dread" (ibid.). She rushes back to the schoolhouse but is too late – her sister is already dead. It takes Lily a long time to get over Helen's death: "When people kill themselves, they think they're ending the pain, but all they're doing is passing it on

to those they leave behind" (pg. 145). In fact, she only really starts to get over it when she decides to have a child of her own, to make up in some way for Helen's baby that died with her.
Perhaps the relationship we learn most about in the story is the one between Lily and her daughter. This relationship is not a particularly easy one as, once again, the characters of the two people involved are completely different. In addition to this, Lily's initial feelings towards her daughter are partly influenced by what happened to Helen. When she sees that Rosemary is a beautiful baby, she does not consider this a good thing: "Helen's beauty, as far as I was concerned, had been a curse, and I resolved that I would never tell Rosemary she was beautiful" (pg. 153). Lily is determined to shape her daughter's character and teach her what is important in life. Unfortunately for her, this does not prove very easy. Rosemary never pays much attention to the many "lessons" Lily wants her to learn, whether these are academic subjects like math and spelling, or 'life lessons', such as the danger of giving animals their freedom. Lily wants to make Rosemary more like her, ignoring her daughter's own interests in the process. For example, although Rosemary is a talented artist and wants to earn her living by painting, Lily does her best to find an alternative career for her. In the end, she gives in up to a point, allowing Rosemary to study art at university, but on condition that she studies to be a teacher at the same time. She does not even have any of her daughter's artwork displayed in her home until Rex forces her to hang up one of Rosemary's pictures. Lily's reason is that Rosemary's work does not match the furnishings – however, this comes across as another example of Lily not taking her daughter seriously. Lily finds it very frustrating that, more often than not, she fails to get her message through to her daughter: "I always liked to think I'd never met a kid I couldn't teach. […] Turns out I was wrong. That kid is you" (pg. 319). In the end, she has to reluctantly accept that Rosemary will continue to do whatever she likes, whether Lily approves or not.

However, their relationship is not all bad. In spite of their very different characters, they have several things in common, such as a love of the outdoor life, of horses, of the beauty of remote areas of the country. When Rosemary describes in a letter how she stood up to a fellow pupil at her boarding school who was being rude about her father, Lily is proud that she has shown such spirit: "Maybe she's got a bit of her mother in her after all" (pg. 239). And, although Rosemary insists on marrying a man that her mother deeply disapproves of, Lily is determined to remain part of her life and to be involved in the raising of her grandchildren. She does not reject her daughter, even though Rosemary did not turn out the way she intended.

Lily makes few female friends in her life – there is little opportunity for her to do so. The only really close friend she ever has is Minnie Hanagan, who she meets in the boarding house in Chicago that they are both living in. Minnie is beautiful, confident, talkative and a lot of fun to be with. Together, they go out dancing, go shopping, even attend political meetings, and spend lots of time talking about all kinds of things. Minnie is a woman that Lily can really relate to, another strong woman. She is therefore distraught at her friend's tragic death; after the funeral, Lily cuts off her long hair as a tribute to Minnie.

4. What are "half-broke horses"?

1. Describe some of the half-broke horses that appear in the story.

2. Why do you think the phrase was chosen as the title of the novel?

1.

In a literal sense, a "half-broke horse" is one that is no longer completely wild, but is not really tame either. Breaking a horse means training it to carry a saddle and a rider on its back. This is the part of training that Lily is responsible for when she helps her father with his carriage horses. It is not so easy to train half-broke horses, as they have already had some human contact, normally having been used by cowboys for a cattle round-up and then set free again. This treatment makes them mistrust humans, although they can be tamed and trained to be good working horses if this is done in the right way. In fact, these horses are very intelligent, and one such half-broke mare becomes Lily's faithful companion once she has been trained. This horse is part of a group given to Lily's father by their neighbor as compensation for shooting Dad's dogs, and Lily immediately feels that this particular mare is something special. She names her Patches, and rides her all the way to Red Lake when she goes there to work as a teacher. Patches stays with the family until they move to Phoenix. She is very old by this time, so Lily gives her to the local Havasupai tribe to spend the rest of her days in the quiet village in which they live.

The second time she goes to teach in Red Lake, Lily is confronted with another half-broke horse. Two of the town's deputies, including Rooster who later becomes her friend, tell her she has to ride their mustang before she can get her paycheck. Lily can see at once what kind of horse she is dealing with: one that has never been trained properly and is therefore bad-tempered and likely to cause trouble for anyone who attempts to ride him. The two deputies anticipate having some fun at Lily's expense by getting her to ride the mustang; of course, the joke is on them, as she knows exactly how to deal with the horse and quickly gets him to obey her. Her skills as a horsewoman gain Lily a lot of respect in the town. She even starts to ride the mustang, Red Devil, in local horse races, often winning a cash prize.

The phrase "half-broke horse" is also applied to people in the novel. The main example of this is Rosemary. Her mother compares her to a half-broke horse because she also has a wild nature: "She was happiest running around out of doors, without a stitch of clothing if I'd let her" (pg. 178). She loves nature of all kinds, especially animals, with whom she seems to feel a special connection, hating the idea of any animal being locked up. However, unlike real horses, Rosemary proves almost impossible to tame. When she is sent away to boarding school, she does not fit in with the other students because of her wild behavior, which of course is far more noticeable there than on the ranch: "what seemed normal in one situation can seem outright peculiar in another" (pg. 238). Rosemary never manages to behave as the nuns at her school would like her to, and suffers from homesickness, longing to return to the freedom of the ranch.

Even there, however, there are times when her behavior is too wild, even for the more relaxed standards that apply there. On one occasion, she and Lily are asked to accompany two women from the Education Board who are visiting the local Havasupai tribe in order to assess the children's state of health and education. One of the guides is a local Havasupai boy, Fidel, who Rosemary has a crush on. First she shocks the two city women by leaping onto Fidel's horse with him and galloping off down to his village in the valley before Lily can protest. Later she scandalizes them by sneaking out of their hut to go for a midnight swim in her underwear with some of the young Indians, including Fidel. Lily is so furious at her daughter's disobedience that she beats Rosemary severely with her belt. In so doing, she is trying to show Rosemary who is in charge, as she would do with a horse: "There was no other way to teach you a lesson" (pg. 261). However, what would probably have worked on a horse does not have the desired effect on her daughter: "All I learned is that when I have children, I'm never going to whip them" (ibid.).

This incident should be a sign for Lily that it will not be possible for her to 'tame' her daughter. However, she keeps trying to do so, and it is not until her daughter is much older that Lily has to admit that "Rosemary hadn't really listened to what I had to say ever since that time we visited the Havasupai and I gave her the whipping for swimming with Fidel Hanna" (pg. 313-314). It is hardly surprising that Rosemary falls in love with a man who is just as wild and unconventional as she is. After their wedding, Lily watches Rosemary and Rex drive away from the reception, "heading out into open country like a couple of half-broke horses" (pg. 322).

2.

The title "Half Broke Horses" may have been chosen for a couple of reasons. For one thing, it represents the theme of horses in general which recurs throughout the story. It reflects one of Lily's talents, that of a horse-breaker: she demonstrates her ability to deal with wild creatures. In addition to this, the title could also be said to represent certain characters in the story, particularly Rosemary. One of the book's major themes is the relationship between Lily and her daughter. In spite of her many attempts, Lily fails to crush Rosemary's wild side and make her behave in the way she would like. When, in the end, Rosemary still insists on going her own way, Lily feels that she has failed as a mother. It is her husband, Jim, who helps her to see that, even if Rosemary is a 'half-broke horse', this is not necessarily a bad thing. It is just the way she is: "People are like animals. [...] Some are happiest penned in, some need to roam free. You got to recognize what's in her nature and accept it" (pg. 320). He points out that Rosemary is happy in the life she has chosen, "so she's way ahead of a lot of folks" (ibid.). In the end, Lily has to see that the one creature she will never tame is her own half-broke horse.

5. Role of teaching

1. *Half Broke Horses* is dedicated to all teachers. Discuss the role of teaching in the novel.

2. What kind of teacher is Lily?

1.

For Lily, education is one of the most important things in life. As well as being very interested in learning, she finds from an early age that she likes teaching and is good at it. She soon feels that becoming a teacher is her "calling" (pg. 56) and her "Purpose" (pg. 57) in life. It is her father who originally sets her out on this path, as he was her first teacher. A man with extensive knowledge of all kinds of subjects, he is able to instill his daughter with a love of learning. In particular, she becomes interested in science subjects, and loves "learning that there were these invisible rules that explained the mysteries of the world we lived in" (pg. 31). Dad's teaching does at times reflect his own bias, however: his take on history has "a decidedly west-of-the-Pecos point of view" (ibid.), for example. In other words, he teaches them that the Mexicans and Native Americans were oppressed by the early English settlers, who he dismisses as "a bunch of pious hypocrites" (ibid.). Lily's father believes that he can provide her with a much better education than the local school, which is why she and her siblings do not go there. However, even if he can give his children a high standard of education, he realizes the importance of having "a piece of paper to prove you got it" (pg. 32), which is why he sends Lily and Buster away to boarding school when they are old enough.

Another teacher who plays an important role in Lily's life is Mother Albertina, the principal of her boarding school. She is the one who first puts the idea of becoming a teacher into Lily's head, making her realize that this would be the ideal career for her because she "loved that 'Eureka!' moment when someone finally figured something out" (pg. 57). Another thing that appeals to her about becoming a teacher is that she would be able to work for herself – even at a young age, she is fiercely independent, and cannot imagine having a boss. Lily is lucky enough to be able to get teaching jobs before she is fully qualified, due to a lack of teachers in remote areas, so quickly has the chance to discover that she does indeed love teaching. She finds it particularly satisfying to make a difference to a child's life, to give them basic skills such as reading, writing and math. Moreover, she is good at her job: "I never met a kid I couldn't teach.

Every kid was good at something, and the trick was to find out what it was, then use it to teach him everything else" (pg. 85). She is well-respected in the small towns in which she teaches, as all of the families, no matter how poor, are eager for their children to get an education and are grateful to her for providing it.

2.

Some of Lily's teaching methods would not be acceptable today. She expects her students to be obedient and respectful at all times, and she uses a willow branch to hit any who are cheeky to her. Her reasoning behind this is that it is important to establish right from the beginning who is in charge: "Kids were like horses in that things went a lot easier if you got their respect from the outset rather than trying to demand it after they'd started seeing what they could get away with" (pg. 119). On the whole, this form of discipline works well, although her own children do not like it when she punishes them in front of the class. Lily feels, however, that it is important for her not to show Rosemary and Little Jim any favoritism, which is why she also forbids them to make friends with any of their fellow pupils. As a result, they do not particularly enjoy having their mother as a teacher.

Although Lily is a good teacher, she often loses her job. This is not always her fault: she is let go from her original job as an itinerant teacher because the First World War has ended and all the original teachers in those towns are returning home. However, there are times when she is fired because she refuses to compromise on her principles. One example of this is when she is teaching in the town of Main Street, a very remote place in which almost all the inhabitants are Mormon polygamists. The families are all related to each other, and the roles for men and women are strictly defined. From a young age, the girls are trained to become wives and mothers, and are only expected to get just about enough education to be able to fulfill these roles: anything more is considered unnecessary. For someone who has had as much life experience as Lily, this is unimaginable. She considers it her duty to teach the children, especially the girls, that there is a world of opportunity out there far beyond being a housewife, and that they can seize these opportunities if they really want to. It is not long before she is visited by one of the elders of the Mormon community, Uncle Eli, who warns her not to put ideas into the girls' heads. He speaks very patronizingly to her, calling her "Teacher Lady" (pg. 210) and telling her that his community wants to stay away from the modern world. Naturally, this attitude annoys Lily, whose response to him is "I don't need you telling me my job. My job is to give these kids an education, and part of that is letting them know a little bit about what the world is really like" (ibid.). Seeing that he is not going to change her mind, Uncle Eli tries to intimidate her instead. One evening, when he keeps knocking on her door and will not leave, she threatens him with her pistol, shooting past his ear as a warning. This leads to a visit from the local sheriff, who tells her that she will have to leave if she is not able to get on with the local people. Typically, Lily refuses to change her teaching methods, and her contract is not renewed for the following school year. She still feels she has acted for the best, and does not regret telling her students about their options, even though she is now unemployed as a result. For her, this is just as important a part of her job as teaching the basics.

6. Lily's two husbands

1. Compare Lily's two husbands. What does she learn from her marriage to Ted Conover?

2. How does it affect her relationship with Jim Smith?

1.

Lily meets her first husband, Ted Conover, just after her friend Minnie is killed. Because Minnie was her only real friend in Chicago, where she is living at the time, she is feeling particularly lonely and is therefore more susceptible to his charms. Ted's happy nature is just what she needs to cheer her up after Minnie's accident. Although the way he does his job, talking his way into people's houses to sell them vacuum cleaners, shows her that he is not completely trustworthy, she cannot help liking him and enjoying his company.

He takes her out to dinner and they have lots of fun together, something that Lily is not really used to. He talks and jokes a lot, making her laugh. Before long, she has agreed to marry him. Being such an independent person, she is quite surprised to find that she enjoys being married and having someone to look after her. One of the things she likes about Ted is that dreams and ambitions are important to him. He encourages her to work towards her dreams of getting a college education and learn to fly a plane, and he himself plans to start his own business. They decide to work hard and save as much money as they can in order to turn these ambitions into reality at some point in the future.

As a traveling vacuum cleaner salesman, Ted is often away for several days at a time, but this does not bother Lily as she has a job during the day and studies at night school in the evenings in order to get her high-school diploma. However, one day she is involved in a car accident and, in the hospital, is told to phone her husband to let him know what has happened. A man at his company tells her that he is not on the road at the moment after all, and that she cannot be his wife because his wife's name is Margaret. At these revelations, Lily's world falls apart. By doing a little detective work, she finds out where Ted's other home is, and discovers that, as well as a wife, he has three children. When Lily confronts Ted, he tries to lie his way out of trouble and play on her sympathy by telling her that she is the one he loves, but she does not believe him. Utterly betrayed, she has the marriage annulled and tries to put it behind her. Although she is strong enough to start again, the experience leaves her with a mistrust of men that she never completely gets over.

2.

Lily is sure that she will never marry again. When she and Jim Smith first become friends, he makes it clear that he would like to take things further, but never says anything specific, and Lily does not raise the subject with him. However, after Helen's death, she feels that she would like to have a child, and to do so she will need a husband. Jim Smith seems the logical choice. She has learnt from her experience with Ted about the kind of man she does not want to be with; fortunately, Jim is different from Ted in almost every way. For one thing, he does not talk needlessly all the time: "He spoke when he had something to say, and if he didn't, he felt no need to fill the void with hot air" (pg. 127). He led an adventurous life in his youth, but is now hard-working, steady and reliable, something that could certainly not be said of Ted. He loves the outdoor life and is happiest doing physical work. Most of all, he is "dependable and established" (pg. 129) and runs an honest business. They have a lot in common, such as a love of horses and cars; both of them are also unafraid of hard work. It is important to Lily that she and Jim are equal partners in marriage. This was certainly not the case with her and Ted: by leading a double life, Ted had an advantage over Lily, making a fool of her by making her believe she was happily married. She is determined not to make the same mistake again.

Jim's calm personality is just what Lily needs. He "never lost his temper" (ibid.) and "always knew what he thought and how he felt" (ibid.). This is a good antidote to Lily's anger and frustration at certain times, such as when she loses one of her teaching jobs simply for standing up for her principles, as she sees it. Moreover, Jim is far more relaxed towards Rosemary, accepting her for who she is rather than trying to change her as Lily does. He is the one who shows her that it is all right for Rosemary to marry Rex instead of choosing a more conventional life. He tries to convince Lily that she has not failed as a mother: "Don't beat yourself up. [...] She might not have turned out like you planned, but that don't mean she turned out wrong" (pg. 320). In his opinion, Rosemary can lead whatever kind of life she likes, as long as she is happy, and he does his best to make Lily see this, too.

However, one thing her marriage to Ted taught her is that she should never trust a man completely. This is why, when the family is living in Phoenix, she starts to suspect that Jim might be having an affair with a co-worker who keeps flirting with him. Although she thinks she knows Jim very well, her experience with Ted has sown a tiny seed of doubt in her mind that she cannot ignore. Therefore she decides to spy on him, enlisting Rosemary's help, to find out if there really is anything going on between him and the woman. It turns out that Jim has always been completely faithful to her, and in fact he shows how much he loves her by suggesting that living in the big city is damaging their relationship, making Lily's imagination run wild. His solution is for them to move back to the countryside where they will all be happier. Unlike Ted, who just pretended to love her, Jim really does have Lily's best interests at heart, and would do anything for her.

7. "Lily's distinctive voice"

Jeannette Walls decided to write her novel in the first person because she wanted to "capture Lily's distinctive voice". Does she succeed in doing so?

Although *Half Broke Horses* describes people and events that really existed, it is written in the style of a novel rather than as a biography. Moreover, Jeannette Walls writes the story of Lily in the first person, allowing her to tell the story of her remarkable life in her own words. This is certainly effective in bringing Lily's character to life, giving us a vivid picture of the kind of person she was.

The language that Lily uses says a lot about the kind of person she is. She is not a person who minces her words. If she has a low opinion of something or someone, she says so: she is a person who tells it like it is. However, she also has a witty way of expressing herself, often using understatement to make her point. Therefore we learn that her mother "wasn't exactly the most useful person in the world" (pg. 34), her father "was never the most practical man in the world" (pg. 51), her sister Helen "was not the most self-reliant creature in the world" (pg. 115) and that Buster "was always a little unmotivated" (pg. 72). In addition to this, she has a habit of giving nicknames to people based on their behavior or personal traits that paints a clear picture of the person she is talking about. Therefore the man who knocks her down with his car in Chicago is referred to as "Slick" (pg. 103) because of his slicked-back hair and the way he is so quick to deny to the passersby that he was the one who caused the accident. The man who buys the ranch she and Jim are running is a Hollywood director who she calls "Gaiters" (pg. 263) because of the slightly ridiculous clothes he is wearing; in addition to this, most of the things he says seem slightly ridiculous, too, especially when he tells them that the ranch does not look like his idea of a ranch and they need to "goose the magic" (pg. 264). Sometimes the nickname even sticks, as in the case of Rooster, who she first refers to by that name because of his appearance, and then continues to call him that to his face as a sign of affection. Overall, her descriptions of people are both vivid and amusing. The language she uses is frequently colorful, reflecting the fact that she was brought up on a ranch rather than in fine society. She frequently refers to her ex-husband as a "crumb bum" (pg. 109), and the way she attacks him when she finds out he has betrayed her can leave him in no doubt about how furious she is: "You no-good low-down dirty lying scum-sucking son of a bitch!" (pg. 107). Clearly, she has never become a lady, as her mother hoped she would.

Nevertheless, it is important to remember that this is not an autobiography, and Lily is in fact speaking through her granddaughter. Jeannette Walls explains in her author's note that she remembers her grandmother well and had a close relationship with her. However, Lily died when Jeannette was eight, so she has learnt most of what she knows about Lily through other people, especially her mother, Rosemary. She has not heard most of the stories from Lily's own lips, and has therefore had to use her imagination to recreate conversations and to allow Lily to voice her opinions. Most of the story is fact rather than fiction, and Lily was a real person rather than someone created by the author. However, Jeannette Walls has had to create Lily's voice to a certain extent as she was no longer around to write down her story herself. Therefore it can perhaps be said that Jeannette has managed to capture what Lily's voice was probably like. With the voice she has given Lily, she manages to convey the fact that she was a unique person, and certainly succeeds in creating an unforgettable character.

Index

B
Buster 5, 8, 10, 12, 16, 23, 29, 52, 80, 85 f., 99, 116 f., 120 f., 139, 146, 152

C
Cars 16, 20 f., 24, 26, 33, 37, 46 f., 51 f., 59, 76, 82, 101, 115, 126 f.
Chicago 13, 17 f., 20 ff., 71, 74, 80, 84, 88, 107, 111 f., 114, 117, 125, 133, 152
Cowboys 12 f., 29, 38 f., 47, 53, 57, 61, 91, 93, 96, 100, 125 f., 143

D
Dad 5 ff., 10 ff., 51 f., 76 f., 81 f., 85, 109, 121, 129, 134 f., 139, 152
- horses 6 f., 17, 80 ff., 124, 127, 137, 143
- as a teacher 7, 71 f., 77, 81, 83, 116, 146

Dorothy 10 ff., 16, 23, 29, 76, 80, 82, 85

G
God and religion 5 ff., 29 f., 80, 97, 105, 120 f., 129, 139
- Mormons 27, 31, 42 ff., 73, 122 f., 147

H
Hackberry Ranch 42 f., 52 f., 57 f., 61, 96, 100, 113
Half-broke horses 11, 24, 39, 50, 67, 94, 98, 104, 124 ff., 143 f.
Helen 5, 16, 23, 27 f., 31 f., 52, 75, 79, 80, 86 f., 93 f., 108, 116 f., 120 ff., 129, 134 f., 140 f., 152
Horses 5, 7, 11 ff., 17, 23 ff., 27 f., 37 ff., 49 f., 54 f., 57 ff., 65 f., 72 f., 77, 80 ff., 89, 93 ff., 98 f., 102, 107, 110, 124 f., 127, 136, 138, 141 ff., 147, 150

J
Jim Smith 23, 26 ff., 30, 36 f., 47 f., 57 f., 65, 67, 89 f., 107 f., 115, 122, 138, 149 f.
- garage owner 32 f., 70, 89, 127, 137
- marriage to Lily 31 f., 61 f., 71, 77, 108, 129
- relationship with Rosemary 40, 54, 66, 92, 93, 120, 145, 150
- working with animals 34 f., 38 f., 60 f., 89, 90, 92, 125

K
KC Ranch 8, 10 f., 13, 16 f., 23, 29, 33, 49, 51 f., 71, 74, 83, 85, 87, 112, 125, 128, 135

L
Lily Casey Smith
- cars and driving 26, 45 ff., 59, 76, 115, 126 f.
- education and learning 7 ff., 22 ff., 71 f., 79, 81, 83, 85, 104 f., 116 f., 122, 136 f., 146
- horses 7, 11 f., 17, 23 ff., 49 f., 65, 72, 80, 84, 107, 124 f., 143 f.
- making and saving money 33 f., 43, 45, 47, 70, 91, 127 ff., 137
- planes 16 f., 43, 47, 66, 91, 103, 126 f.
- relationship with her father 10, 17, 51 f., 77, 83 f., 139
- relationship with Helen 27 f., 75, 86 f., 139
- relationship with Jim 31 f., 61 f., 77, 91, 107, 150 f.

- relationship with her mother 6, 23, 75, 79, 80, 139
- relationship with Rosemary 39 f., 48 ff., 53, 56, 59 ff., 64 f., 69, 74 ff., 78, 93 f., 98, 103 f., 118, 120, 126, 130, 134 f., 138, 141
- teacher 7, 13, 15, 43 f., 47 f., 51, 60, 63, 72 f., 83, 105, 116 f., 123, 125, 136 f., 143, 146 f.
- teaching her children a lesson 39 f., 46, 56, 73 f., 98, 119 f., 134 f., 141, 144

Little Jim 32 ff., 36, 41, 44, 46 f., 49 ff., 53, 58, 63 f., 67, 99 f., 116, 119, 147

M

Mom 5 ff., 12, 16, 23, 51, 75, 78 f., 86, 109, 120 f., 129, 134, 136, 139, 152
Mother Albertina 9 f., 12, 72, 76, 104 f., 136, 146
Minnie 13, 18 f., 21, 76, 87, 105 f., 114, 141 f., 149

P

Phoenix 50 f., 58 f., 63, 67 f., 73, 77, 89, 90, 94, 97, 100, 102, 111, 113, 115, 118, 125, 128, 138, 143
Planes 16 f., 43, 47, 59, 66, 91, 92, 103, 126 f.
Playing the cards you've been dealt 52, 121 f., 129 f.
Poms 30, 38, 42, 49, 57

R

Ranch life 37 f., 42 f., 53 f, 57, 109 f., 138 f.
Red Lake 112, 122, 125, 128
- first teaching job 13 ff., 71, 143
- second stint as a teacher 23 ff., 28, 31, 77, 107, 117, 143
- meeting her second husband 26 f., 32, 89

Rex Walls 63 ff., 67 f., 78, 89, 92, 96, 97 f., 100 f., 120, 126, 128, 131, 135, 141, 144, 150
Rooster 24 f., 28, 30, 36, 77, 107 f., 122, 125, 143, 152

Rosemary 32, 34, 36, 40, 41, 45, 47, 51, 61 f., 92 f., 115, 118 f., 131, 153
- artist 42, 51, 59 f., 64, 67, 96 f., 141
- love of animals 35, 39, 49 f., 53 f., 59, 65, 97, 99, 125, 134 f., 144
- and Rex 63 f., 68, 96 f., 98, 100 f., 104, 120, 126, 135
- schooling 44, 46, 50, 63 f., 76, 95, 116 f., 119, 141, 144, 147
- wild nature 39, 50 f., 54 f., 75, 93 f., 96, 101, 126, 144

S

Salt Draw 5 f., 8, 49, 52 f., 71, 78, 79, 110 ff., 122

T

Ted Conover 19 f., 87 f., 89, 114, 129, 137, 149 f.

W

Water 17 f., 30, 32, 37 f., 41 f., 55, 91, 99, 109 f., 114
- drought 41 f., 110
- floods 5 f., 30, 41, 70, 110, 120 f., 138
- storms 40 f., 99, 110

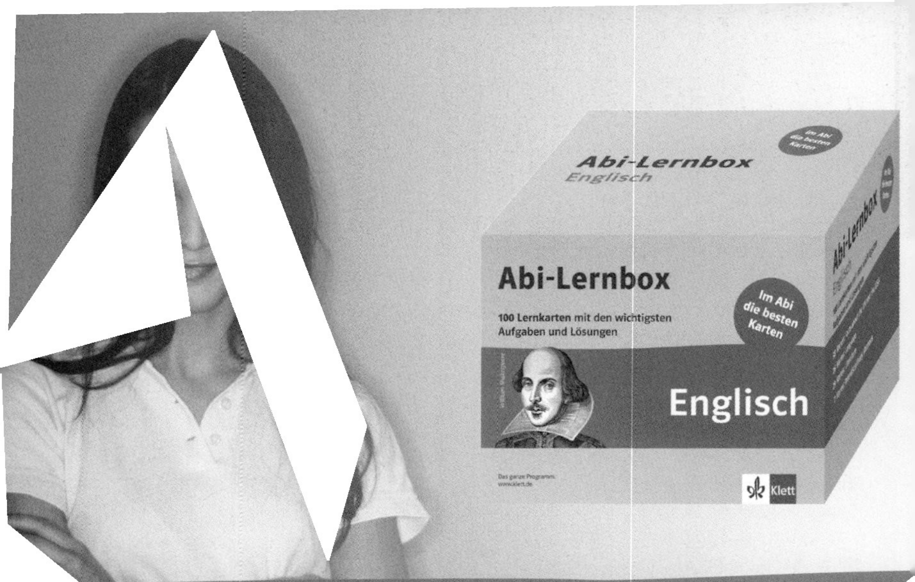

Die besten Karten im Abi

Die ersten Lernkarten fürs Abitur mit den 100 wichtigsten Aufgaben, die man im Abitur beherrschen muss. Die Karteikarten im A6-Format beinhalten Aufgaben, Lösungen und, auf der aufklappbaren Innenseite, ausführliches Wissen zum jeweiligen Thema.

ADDITIONAL INFORMATION 15

English | Facts about the UK and the USA | The Main Parties in the USA

The Democrats

Party emblem (often used in cartoons):

the donkey

Having established themselves as the party of social reform and progress in the past, the Democrats generally advocate

- heavily taxing the rich and large enterprises to finance welfare programmes for the socially disadvantaged,
- affirmative action as a means of fighting racial inequality,
- diplomacy over military action,
- crime prevention,
- a more efficient health care system.

Among the Democrats there is a growing awareness of the importance of environmental protection. Their more liberal stand on questions such as

- abortion,
- same-sex marriages and
- stem-cell research

which appeal to intellectuals, but among their supporters are also working-class people, members of minorities and unions.

Abi-Lernbox Englisch

100 Lernkarten mit den wichtigsten Aufgaben und Lösungen

ISBN978-3-12-929971-5 | 19,95 Euro

Bertolt Brecht
Der gute Mensch von Sezuan
ISBN 978-3-12-923081-7

Bertolt Brecht
Leben des Galilei
ISBN 978-3-12-923066-4

Friedrich Dürrenmatt
Der Besuch der alten Dame
ISBN 978-3-12-923054-1

Georg Büchner
Dantons Tod
ISBN 978-3-12-923073-2

Georg Büchner
Woyzeck
ISBN 978-3-12-923005-3

Friedrich Dürrenmatt
Die Physiker
ISBN 978-3-12-923079-4

Theodor Fontane
Effi Briest
ISBN 978-3-12-923029-9

Max Frisch
Andorra
ISBN 978-3-12-923075-6

Max Frisch
Homo faber
ISBN 978-3-12-923061-9

Johann Wolfgang von Goethe
Faust – Erster Teil
ISBN 978-3-12-923063-3

Johann Wolfgang von Goethe
Iphigenie auf Tauris
ISBN 978-3-12-923062-6

Johann Wolfgang von Goethe
Die Leiden des jungen Werther
ISBN 978-3-12-923006-0

Gerhart Hauptmann
Die Ratten
ISBN 978-3-12-923049-7

E.T.A. Hoffmann
Der Sandmann
ISBN 978-3-12-923071-8

Franz Kafka
Der Proceß
ISBN 978-3-12-923023-7

Franz Kafka
Die Verwandlung
ISBN 978-3-12-923077-0

Heinrich von Kleist
Michael Kohlhaas
ISBN 978-3-12-923024-4

Heinrich von Kleist
Die Marquise von O. / Das Erdbeben in Chili
ISBN 978-3-12-923055-8

Heinrich von Kleist
Prinz Friedrich von Homburg
ISBN 978-3-12-923056-5

Wolfgang Koeppen
Tauben im Gras
ISBN 978-3-12-923051-0

Gotthold Ephraim Lessing
Emilia Galotti
ISBN 978-3-12-923074-9

Gotthold Ephraim Lessing
Nathan der Weise
ISBN 978-3-12-923068-8

Liebeslyrik
ISBN 978-3-12-923031-2

Lyrik der Nachkriegszeit 1945 – 1960
ISBN 978-3-12-923013-8

Thomas Mann
Buddenbrooks
ISBN 978-3-12-923058-9

Thomas Mann
Mario und der Zauberer / Tonio Kröger
ISBN 978-3-12-923059-6

Joseph Roth
Hiob
ISBN 978-3-12-923076-3

Neue Sachlichkeit
ISBN 978-3-12-923052-7

Friedrich Schiller
Kabale und Liebe
ISBN 978-3-12-923065-7

Friedrich Schiller
Maria Stuart
ISBN 978-3-12-923078-7

Friedrich Schiller
Die Räuber
ISBN 978-3-12-923026-8

Bernhard Schlink
Der Vorleser
ISBN 978-3-12-923070-1

Peter Stamm
Agnes
ISBN 978-3-12-923072-5

Patrick Süskind
Das Parfum
ISBN 978-3-12-923064-0

Lektürehilfen – Literatur verstehen

Lektürehilfen sind der Schlüssel zum besseren Verständnis von Literatur:

- Die wichtigen Themen kennen dank thematischer Kapitel.
- Die richtigen Antworten wissen durch die Vorbereitung mit typischen Abiturfragen.
- Inhaltsangabe der Lektüre als mp3-Download unter: www.klett.de/lernhilfen

Paul Haggis
ISBN 978-3-12-923083-1 | 9,99 €

Paul Auster
Moon Palace
ISBN 978-3-12-923046-6 | 9,95 €

T. C. Boyle
Tortilla Curtain
ISBN 978-3-12-923001-5 | 9,95 €

Ray Bradbury
Fahrenheit 451
ISBN 978-3-12-923050-3 | 9,95 €

Caught between Cultures
ISBN 978-3-12-923016-9 | 9,95 €

Don DeLillo
Falling Man
ISBN 978-3-12-923053-4 | 9,95 €

Nick Hornby
About a Boy
ISBN 978-3-12-923003-9 | 9,95 €

Arthur Miller
Death of a Salesman
ISBN 978-3-12-923048-0 | 9,95 €

Willy Russell
Educating Rita
ISBN 978-3-12-923028-2 | 9,95 €

William Shakespeare
Romeo and Juliet
ISBN 978-3-12-923039-8 | 9,95 €

Macbeth
ISBN 978-3-12-923038-1 | 9,95 €

Tennessee Williams
A Streetcar Named Desire
ISBN 978-3-12-923045-9 | 9,95 €